M000087392

THE

MAKING OF AMERICA
SERIES

CEDARBURG
A HISTORY SET IN STONE

This photo won many an award for the photographer, Harold Dobberpuhl. It also depicts the timeless quality of Cedarburg that made its downtown a candidate for the National Register of Historic Places. When the city succeeded in gaining protected status, it ensured that future generations would have a touchstone to the past, that tomorrow's children would have a reference point when planning their future. (Photo by Harold Dobberpuhl.)

THE
MAKING OF AMERICA
SERIES

CEDARBURG
A HISTORY SET IN STONE

RYAN GIERACH

ARCADIA
PUBLISHING

Copyright © 2003 by Ryan Gierach
ISBN 978-1-58973-165-3

Published by Arcadia Publishing
Charleston, South Carolina

For all general information contact Arcadia Publishing at:
Telephone 843-853-2070
Fax 843-853-0044
E-Mail sales@arcadiapublishing.com
For customer service and orders:
Toll-Free 1-888-313-2665

Visit us on the Internet at www.arcadiapublishing.com

Front cover: *Cedarburg in the late 1940s celebrated prosperity as it had always feted anything—there was a parade. Oftentimes, there were so many marchers and bandsmen in the parade that few people stood on the sidewalk to watch the procession. None seemed to mind. (Photo by Harold Dobberpuhl.)*

CONTENTS

Acknowledgments   6

Foreword   7

1.   Pre-White Settlement   10

2.   New Dublin   20

3.   Of Rock, Water, and Germans   27

4.   Father Hilgen and Company   39

5.   From Forest, a Teutonic Village   52

6.   Panic, War, Riot, and the Iron Horse   69

7.   A Teutonic Utopia Realized   84

8.   The Gilded-German Age Gives Way to the American Century   105

9.   Depression, War, Boom   123

10. The "City with a Stone Face" Becomes an American Gemstone   140

Bibliography   156

Index   159

ACKNOWLEDGMENTS

The professional level of historical investigation in Cedarburg impressed me as I cobbled together this book. These incredible men and women did the real work on which I base this history. I thank them all for their gracious assistance. Thank you Ed Rappold for your unflinching support, both in checking the text and opening your photographic collection. Thanks also Bob Armbruster for your friendship, your patience, for checking the historical accuracy of the text, and for the liberal use of your archive. And thank you Carl Edquist for opening to me your wife's amazing legacy—the Rita Edquist Collection.

To the Cedarburg Cultural Center, thank you for your more than gracious support. Joan Dobberpuhl, who offered so much assistance to me in the wake of her husband Harold's passing, deserves special thanks. Gus "Sandy" Wirth, you're the best. Bill Ritter, Harry Wiegert, Bob Fuller, Tomi Faye Forbes, Mayor Jim Coutts, Allen "Tubby" Boerner, Jim Pape, Tony Fischer, this wouldn't have happened without you. Al Rempel and Curt Gruenwald, thank you for opening the Ozaukee County Historical Society's Pioneer Village for me during the winter. To the Cedarburg Public Library's Mary Marquardt and Gail Skiff—your enthusiasm about the project excited me. Thank you also to the Wisconsin State Historical Society's staff. Thank you all whom I fail to mention by name.

To my cousin Pam Boesch and her husband Bob for their gracious hospitality; thank you. Kevin, my brother, thank you for your support and encouragement. Liz Mann and Jim Rudolph, your friendship and encouragement (not to mention your editing help) stands unsurpassed. Thomas Halstead, a finer and better friend can't be had. Marcus Fant—how do I even describe how important you are to me? I find myself without words. And thank you especially Chuck Edwards; you've made a dream come true.

FOR MY MOTHER, MARY LOUISE GIERACH,
AND FOR TRACY SYPERT,
WHO WATCHES WITH GLEE FROM BEYOND.

FOREWORD

Not to have knowledge of what happened before you were born is to be condemned to live forever as a child.

–Cicero

You were curious enough about Cedarburg's history to pick up this book and take a look at the jacket and inquisitive enough to open it to the foreword. Or perhaps, you've already bought the book. In either case I offer you my heartfelt thanks. It proves that you share my interest about the unique and singular town of Cedarburg. Hopefully reading these pages will satisfy your curiosity as much as writing them did mine.

I have always been interested in history, perhaps because I have always yearned to travel yet was unable to afford it. Virginia Woolf once wrote, "Whoever said that the past is another country was right." So I fulfilled my desire to see the world by journeying to distant lands and visiting strange and wonderful people by reading historical accounts.

In the summer of 2001, I spent an extended vacation in my hometown attending my high school class reunion. This first long visit home in 25 years was to a place I couldn't wait to get away from in my youth, a place I considered to be a stodgy farm town. I had landed then in Los Angeles, where I worked and prospered in the world of commerce before leaving for academia to attend UCLA and study history (mostly tenth- and eleventh-century Norman history). This path led me to a career as a freelance writer for national and regional periodicals.

When I left the "Burg" in the late 1970s, the town had only just discovered its sense of history, and tourism had not yet taken hold. So sleepy a town was Cedarburg that I felt one could fire a cannon down Washington Avenue from St. Francis Borgia without endangering life. The change I discovered during my 2001 visit honestly stunned me. No matter what day, what time, or where I traveled in town, I saw tourists gazing at the stone buildings I had always taken for granted. I saw people popping into and out of shops; I saw groups walking with docents learning about the architecture and history of Cedarburg.

I mention taking the buildings for granted as a youth because in Los Angeles, a land where people re-invent themselves, architecture and buildings are recreated as often as the inhabitants. Comedian Steve Martin, in his movie *LA Story*, while trying to impress a British woman, declares " . . . and some of these buildings are more than *25 years old!*" That Cedarburg summer I began to truly understand the importance of those beautiful old buildings. To me they came to represent the essence of what a nineteenth-century American city was, much as Los Angeles stands as the quintessential contemporary one.

As I walked the downtown of Cedarburg that summer, visiting the stairs at the creek from which I played as a child, I was impressed with how solidly downtown stood with its stone and brick buildings, not to mention its ever-so-German neatness. I became curious about a history that I had never been the slightest bit interested in, that of how this town had come to be and how it came to be protected.

A quick visit to the local library demonstrated that while some conscientious souls had constructed something of an assortment of histories about their beloved home, no comprehensive book-length edition had yet been attempted. I became determined to write it, not realizing that in the process I would rediscover my roots.

We historians know that growing up in a place, especially a town as distinctive and unique as Cedarburg, makes one irrevocably *of* that place. We also know being away from there for a time makes one not only more appreciative of that beginning, but also able to approach the subject matter with an objectivity those

The east corner of Washington Avenue (Main Street) and Columbia Avenue, depicted here in 2003, has looked exactly the same for over 80 years. One never finds litter or trash, let alone a flower out of place, in Cedarburg.

living in the community cannot possess. I recently read a history of a Wisconsin town done by the head of the city's historical society. He admitted avoiding controversial or "seamy" subjects, saying *his* history "is not the book for that sort of thing." Perhaps he feared facing the descendants of those he would have exposed, or maybe he felt a moral compunction not to speak ill of the dead, but it is obvious that he had ignored the primary responsibility of a historian—being objective. Historians tell the story of what happened, but most importantly, they help clarify what it means to us today.

Much of what I am, for good or ill, was shaped by the culture, traditions, and Gemutlichkeit Conservatism (good times conservatism) of Cedarburg, and by its citizen's competent and realistic approach to life's problems. I was impressed with how German immigration in Cedarburg compared to the typical migration of immigrants to Wisconsin and how it affected the schools and churches, as well as the social and commercial life; I was interested in determining how it shaped a peculiar kind of citizenry, one which is manifested in the vast accomplishments and hardy prosperity of today's Cedarburg. In fact, while writing this history I learned as much about myself as I did about Cedarburg, and more about what it means to be a product of that German upbringing than I could ever have learned on the West Coast. I suppose you could say that the farm town I couldn't leave soon enough had never left me.

By writing a history of Cedarburg, I learned that German speakers built a Teutonic Utopia along the wild shores of my Cedar Creek. Not one self-consciously constructed, as were those failed utopian communities that sprang up across America in the same era, but one based on a blend of the Teuton tradition of church, hearth, home, and the settlers' deep desire and respect for freedom—a freedom to think, believe, and act as they wished. The rock-walled evidence of that utopian ideal stands today. *A history set in stone.*

Only seven blocks long, downtown is one of the most homogenous collections of stone and brick buildings in the country. Virtually every one of these was built before 1920. They were constructed for the ages, an indication that those settlers and civic leaders who created Cedarburg knew full well they had built a society on traditions as rock-solid as the stones with which they built their shelter.

I offer this history as a way to honor that tradition, and I thank Messrs. Hilgen, Schroeder, Groth, Ritter, Fischer, and all the others who created and maintained a community of high ideals in a tamed wilderness, one which made me the man I am.

Upon embarking on a book, every writer makes plans to include anything remotely related to the topic, or they declare "I won't leave that out . . . or this." Yet I must confess I didn't include some tidbits and did leave out a few morsels. Hopefully, the people who notice such things will forgive my choices, for as much as I wanted this to be a comprehensive history, the book I imagined was too large for my publisher. I instead attempted to portray and explain the story of Cedarburg and its importance in this vast cultural landscape of America. I can only hope that I was successful with that goal, and so I humbly put forth this book to honor the idea of Cedarburg, an idea set in stone.

1. Pre-White Settlement

I came to the emigrants' home; echoes from the voice of civilization begat each other in the shady wood and lent their music to the prairie wind.

–Author unknown

The idyllic place that is Cedarburg, a swiftly descending creek on a bend, a forested woodland on rolling moraine near a protective Great Lake, existed for millennia before any European viewed it, civilized it, or even imagined it. The land lay untouched by humans until 12,000 years ago, just after the last retreating glaciers had planed down the Niagara limestone bedrock, creating a generally level but sloping surface descending to Lake Michigan.

Those geologic forces shaped the land long before man arrived; glaciers created a bountiful landscape; and the climate provided four seasons with ample flora and fauna. From the lakeshore, the land rises an average of 12 feet per mile in a succession of glacial ridges moving west, eventually cresting at the state's watershed between the Mississippi and Menomonee/Milwaukee tributaries 10 miles west of Ozaukee County. These discontinuous glacial ridges create a rolling surface one could call "hilly" in north to south ridges parallel to the lakeshore. South flowing streams drain the lowlands between.

The waterways that spring from this watershed left the land well-irrigated and lush, with aquifers beneath the limestone and numerous fresh springs providing excellent drinking water. The Milwaukee River touches Ozaukee County near Saukville, leaves and returns through Fredonia, southeast through Saukville, then south parallel to the lake through Grafton and Mequon.

Yet it is Cedar Creek that gave shape to the township, village, and city of Cedarburg. It is that creek, Milwaukee River's largest tributary rising in Washington County at Big Cedar Lake, that gave the town its birth and sustenance and formed its present topography.

A deep human past, the period 12,000–3,000 years ago, when Asiatic immigrants arrived to chase down mastodon and musk oxen on the freshly scrubbed glacial hillsides, is a nearly complete mystery to us. A few flint spear tips, beads, and fluted axes provide evidence that the people did indeed live in the area. Yet only with the advent of pottery shards left by these Paleo-Indians beginning around 1000

Cedar Creek snakes and dances through Cedarburg, dropping 80 feet in less than 2 miles. This spot is below the Milldam and in a city park. (Photo by Harold Dobberpuhl.)

B.C. do we begin to get a picture of their lives. When the culture that developed began to build mounds about 1,500 years ago, that picture became more clear. It turns out that southern Wisconsin (and southeastern Wisconsin in particular) was the center of what anthropologists call the Effigy Mound Culture, a culture seemingly preoccupied with the building of large earthen works.

Many of these are burial mounds, but by no means all. The meaning of the mounds has disappeared along with the mound builders, for they left no written record. Anthropologists and archeologists suggest that the mounds were either religious/ceremonial structures or a means to organize and control their nascent society, or both. The massive structures would have taken many thousands of man-hours and months of time as men and women alike carried woven reed baskets filled with soil and then packed it into shape. The "social organizationalists" point to sites that often had mathematic organization— squares, octagons, and circles—as a proof of their theory.

However, the anthropologists who believe that the aborigines built to celebrate their reverence for the land and the nature that gave them life and sustenance point out that Wisconsin mound builders did something "special," something not seen outside the state—they built imitative mounds of snakes, or birds, reptiles or fish, beasts, even trees and man himself. Called "animal mounds," they represent an advancement of the idea of mound building and, to these experts, a symbolic honoring of the natural resources that meant survival, even prosperity, to these people.

11

Ample evidence exists that Cedarburg and the surroundings were once major mound builder settlements, a natural supposition given the available water for fishing and the great number of fruit and nut-bearing trees, not to mention abundant game. Mounds have been found in and around Cedarburg; one stands on the Klug farm along the Milwaukee River. The land nearest downtown and between Grafton and Cedarburg was mostly used by these people as a hunting ground. The confluence of creek and river, as well as the many natural springs, made the area naturally alluring for wildlife, and of course the hunter. Animal life, even then, knew to avoid large gatherings of men and the Native Americans left the watering areas vacant so they could readily "harvest" the meat.

Anthropologists debate precisely which native tribes followed on the heels of this Effigy Mound Building culture, although it can be said with some confidence that the Winnebago (from whom we get the name of the popular modern-day vacation conveyance) controlled the area at the time of the first white explorer's visit in 1634. Extensive evidence exists that Wisconsin Indians traded with the Arizona and Gulf of Mexico tribes that had contact with white explorers during the previous century. Therefore, brass kettles and glass beads were items of familiarity to the "savages" when Jean Nicolet landed at Green Bay and scouted the shores of Lake Michigan and the Fox River.

That visit foreshadowed disaster for the Native Americans, especially the Winnebago (now usually called the Ho-Chunk). Whether European diseases such as cholera, small pox, measles, typhoid, and scarlet fever were brought up the Mississippi from the south or through the Great Lakes from the east, they spread like wildfire on a windy and parched prairie with a defenseless Native American population. Within 30 years of Nicolet's visit, the Ho-Chunk's population of tens of thousands was reduced to mere hundreds. Other tribes suffered similar fates; estimates of Indian mortality from disease between 1550 and 1700 run as high as 90 percent.

Another disaster befell the population—European-style commercial activity. Where once the tribes had lived a hunting/gathering lifestyle by migrating up and down their hunting areas, they were now employed fur gatherers to feed the Europeans' incredible appetite for pelts. This changed the native economy in profound ways. They no longer hunted for food, but for beaver and fox. Money began to replace barter in the societies. And the worst of it came when the Europeans used the tribes as proxies with which to fight their wars.

Two fur centers dominated the North American continent, the French in Montreal and the Dutch (later the English) in Albany, New York. By 1640, the immediate area around Lakes Huron and Erie had been "furred out," spurring natives and explorers both to look beyond, causing Nicolet to come to Wisconsin while initiating the Iroquois, a Dutch proxy tribe, to expand its territory as far as Michigan and Illinois in the search for furs. Using European-supplied muskets and shot, the Iroquois made war to remove other tribes, pushing them off land that they had held for centuries. This, as one can well imagine, caused a great migration of refugees. With no Red Cross or United Nations at the time, the

Native Americans warred among themselves long before the white man came, causing minor dislocations. However, after the European introduction of steel blades and guns in the mid-seventeenth century, the power balance shifted and a great Indian diaspora resulted, causing many scenes of destitution such as this one. (Courtesy of the Wisconsin State Historical Society.)

emigres went where they could find sustenance, and stumbled upon a then nearly vacant Wisconsin.

In 1664, 30 years after the first white men appeared in the area, the Miami and Menominee tribes replaced the Ho-Chunk in southeastern Wisconsin, moving over for yet another wave of refugees, the Potawatomi tribe, by 1679, when missionaries first mention them. Menomonee Indians retook the area east of the Milwaukee River from the Potawatomi before 1820, migrating slowly southward from their original lands around Green Bay. The French and Indian War from 1754 to 1759 (a commercial war for control of the fur trade and fought primarily by Indians against Indians) drove tens of thousands of Native Americans out of their homelands and into Wisconsin and Minnesota. As a result, Wisconsin became for a time in the eighteenth century the most populous and diverse native territory on the continent, with new additions struggling to survive alongside older populations.

The Fox, Ottawa, Sauk, Kickapoo, Mascouten, and Chippewa newcomers appeared to live side-by-side with the Menominee and Potawatomi tribes on equal footing, blending together and blurring tribal distinctions, while laying claim to lands generally west of the Milwaukee River. The tribes, as different as Poles were from the French and Germans from Italians, found that they had some things in common beside mutual depredation by the Iroquois—a language (all spoke dialects of Algonquin) and a history of intertribal cooperation (the Potawatomi, the Chippewa, and the Ottawa were known in legend as the "Three Fires" for their wartime alliances). But among these tribes of equals, the Potawatomi were first on the scene and therefore had a higher standing, taking much of the land stretching from Door County down the lakeshore to Illinois for their own. In the process, it appears they struck up neighborly relations with the Menominee, still the dominant tribe in north and east Wisconsin.

This was the situation that Rene Robert Cavelier, Seiur de LaSalle, and Father Hennipen found when they, along with 12 other Frenchmen, came to the area in September 1679 to christianize the Indians in conjunction with establishing trading and military posts. However, on the journey the small band was driven ashore by bad weather while on the Milwaukee River at the confluence of Cedar Creek near Grafton. Potawatomi tribesmen lent the wayfarers their gracious assistance on Potawatomi land.

Historical mentions of white men living amidst the Indian populations include Nicolas "Little Corn" Parrot, who lived in the area for 30 years between 1668 and 1698, gaining even the respect of the normally hostile Fox tribe. A missionary Jesuit named Joseph Marest lived for a time at the mouth of the Sauk Creek in Port Washington in 1698, where his cross was found a year later by another missionary. One could suggest that he visited the tribes along Cedar Creek and the Milwaukee River, thus laying reasonable claim to being the first white man to set foot in Cedarburg proper.

The natives these white men lived among now enjoyed a mix of furring and a hunter/gatherer lifestyle, migrating with the season along a wide swath of land from south to north. They fished and hunted bear, deer, moose, elk, caribou, and the occasional buffalo. Fruits, nuts, and berries rounded out their diet, along with harvesting small crops of corn, beans, and squash. These Native Americans tapped the abundant maple trees for syrup, which they boiled down to a sugar. They even smoked homegrown tobacco, or mixed it with bark and leaves to create "Kinnickinnick." They traded maple sugar for sea shells and other exotic products with tribes as far away as California and Florida, with whom the Potowotami also communicated their fears of white encroachment.

The Mascouten tribe has a myth explaining how the Indian trails developed that made trade and communication possible:

> Wisaka, a great killer of serpents, brought down the wrath of the underworld serpents, who tried to kill him. Learning that Wisaka was immortal, they decided to kill his brother Yapatao instead. To get Wisaka out of the way they challenged him to a race around Lake Michigan against a young buffalo. When the pair were on the other side of the lake the serpents attacked Yapatao, who shrieked in rage and anger. Hearing his brother's distress on the winds, Wisaka sped up and returned, only to

find his brother dead. Mourning, he retaliated by killing all the snakes. The trail Wisaka and the buffalo made in their race and on his return remained as Indian trails.

Today these trails are the highways and freeways on which we snake to work.

These Potawatomi and Menominee lived side-by-side in peace near Cedarburg, each on their side of the Milwaukee River, until both gave up claim in the 1830s and moved west and north.

Politically speaking, the territory of Wisconsin did not yet exist. Only when the new American Congress approved the peace treaty negotiated by Benjamin Franklin in Paris, and the United States (then numbering 13) gained their independence from Great Britain on April 15, 1783, did the area containing Wisconsin gain a name—the Northwest Territory. Soon, as pioneers hacked their way through the western wilderness it became the Indiana Territory (1800–1809), the Illinois Territory (1809–1818), and then the Michigan Territory with the name "Michigan west of Lake Michigan."

In October 1818, then-territorial governor Honorable Lewis Cass organized Brown County where the boundaries were set to the current north and east boundaries of the state, and the western border was a straight line drawn north from the Illinois territorial line straight through Portage to the northern boundary. The Menominee held their land as sovereign until 1831, when by treaty they

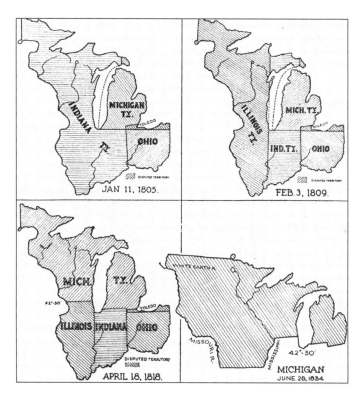

The Northwest Territory, from which Wisconsin emerged as a territory in 1832 to become a state in 1848, went through several political perturbations. Shown here are several maps that outline the different names that Wisconsin had in the early nineteenth century. (Courtesy of the Wisconsin State Historical Society.)

15

negotiated the lands east of the Milwaukee River away to the white man. In 1833, the lands west of the river (Cedarburg) were granted to the United States by the Potawatomi and the Chippewa, but both tribes were given three years after ratification in 1835 to withdraw.

Discovery of lead in Mineral Point (west and south of Madison near Iowa) in 1822 set off the Blackhawk War. Miners were digging for the substance on land Indians held the title to, angering Red Bird, the Winnebago chief. He and a war party attacked and killed some settlers and miners, setting off retaliation from the surrounding forts—Fort Crawford at Prairie Du Chein, Fort Winnebago at Portage, and Fort Howard at Green Bay. By the end of the war, Chief Red Bird's Winnebago tribe, once numbering 1,000, boasted only 150. It was the last armed Native-American conflict in Wisconsin.

Afterward, a great council was formed during which all the tribes with land holdings decided to treat with the white man and eventually cede the lands in Wisconsin to the settlers. They were promised 10¢ an acre by the federal government, a payment some tribes never saw. The Menominee ceded their lands (east of the river) in 1831 and the Potawatomi did the same (those west of the Milwaukee River) in 1838, thus clearing the way for the settlement of Cedarburg.

Red Bird and his tribe of Winnebagos were defeated by Illinois and Wisconsin forces after rising up against miners' incursions into their territory in western Wisconsin. This illustration depicts the U.S. Army battling Red Bird's warriors. (Courtesy of the Wisconsin State Historical Society.)

And so only a few remnants of past Potawatomi tribes, of Chippewa, of Menomonee, Sauk, and Fox, still lived in the area when white settlers entered around 1840. The sparseness of these populations in a land rich with natural resources begs the question of how that could come to be? Yet when one considers the effects of disease, emigration, and the fur trade (along with the accompanying effects of alcohol, or firewater, and the societal changes wrought by a newfound reliance on Western-made manufactured tools, etc.), it became clear that the aboriginal community was one in crisis, and frankly, no longer viable, even on the fringes of Western expansion. No longer did they know or practice the woodcraft as once they had, or sustain the tribal and community cohesion that made them such a vital force in the region. It was a people in diaspora, a culture in chaos, and their way of life was being crippled under the high tide of European invasion, causing them to slip into insignificance.

When the settlers began arriving in even small numbers, the few Indians who stayed must have been very curious about the European lifestyle. Yet they were never a threat to the settlers in southeastern Wisconsin; they were actually more of a nuisance. Many stories exist of how they would walk into a house uninvited to warm themselves on a chilly day, laughing and talking among themselves about the woman of the log house in their own language or how the scent of the baking of bread in the Cedarburg night air (bread was baked overnight in the cooling oven after the other foods were cooked during the day) drew the natives to the source of the fragrant temptation, where they would help themselves to bread from those outdoor "summer" ovens. In exchange, they would gratefully leave nuts and/or berries. You see, Native Americans had never learned to bake (something since rectified), and the smell and taste drew them to fresh baked bread in a way that beggared the imaginations of white settlers.

The territorial whittling and redefining by the new white rulers continued to grow while the Indians removed themselves from the equation. Surveyors were busily measuring and delineating the territory by 1833, discovering that the land was eminently suitable for settlement. S.C. Stambaugh, Indian agent at Green Bay in 1831, described the area between Chicago (then Fort Dearborn) and Green Bay in a report to the federal government:

> . . . at least 2/3 of it is fit for cultivation and offers attractions to the agriculturalist rarely to be found in any country. The soil presents every indication of great fertility; it appears to be a mixture of brown loam and marl, very deep; and whenever its properties have been tested has been found [to be] uncommonly productive.

Stambaugh's account and the accounts of the Sauk War of 1832 heightened interest in an area of the great Northwestern Territory once thought to be uninhabitable. At the same time, agricultural and commercial potential of the land, described in news reports and accentuated by the 1825 completion of the Erie Canal (making it possible to ship grains by water from the Northwest

This is an example of the outdoor "summer ovens" erected by the first settlers in the Northwest Territory. Built with fieldstone, the wood-burning oven and cauldron would get quite hot during the day's use. The final task of the pioneer woman's day was leaving the bread dough to bake in the cooling ovens over night. Others would often be drawn to the scent, "liberate" some bread, and leave behind fruit or nuts in payment.

Territory over the Great Lakes and through to New York City and beyond) created agitation for rapid surveying of the land and for liberal land sale policies. The Erie Canal would prove to be a valuable resource in both directions, as the vast majority of immigrants to Wisconsin used that water route to emigrate instead of the torturous overland route when journeying to their new homes in the Wisconsin wilderness. Later in the late nineteenth century, and due mainly to the splendid and efficient combination of rail and water transport through the Great Lakes and Erie Canal, Wisconsin became the greatest wheat exporting region the world had ever seen.

Advantages of the land to the early European settlers were many and self-evident. The entire state, and the area especially around Cedarburg, was well-watered, drained efficiently, and had fertile soil and abundant forests. For the time period it provided adequate water transportation routes to the Great Lakes and beyond, including extensive water-power and the vast potential for mill sites. And its climate, by European standards, was optimal. The federal land surveys begun in 1833 were the first and most important step in making information on the land available, and the land itself was put up for sale to far off peoples. The settlement door was now open and left ajar, bringing an influx of mostly Yankee settlers at that time.

Political and social events were moving swiftly during this period, causing Congress to create the separate Territory of Wisconsin on April 20, 1836. In December of that year, the new territorial legislature created Washington County out of Milwaukee County, and the legislature also assigned Washington City (later named Port Washington) as the county seat.

All this movement of county lines and seats later had a real impact on the people who would come to inhabit what was at this time utter wilderness and completely devoid of white settlers. In the Western Historical Company's publication *History of Washington and Ozaukee Counties, Wisconsin*:

> An act passed in 1840 contain[ing] a clause which became the root of the trouble finally leading to the establishment of Ozaukee County. That clause, attached to a bill for the organization of Washington County for civil purposes, repealed the provision of 1836 that the county seat be located permanently at the mouth of the Sauk Creek and substituted therefore one which provided that the qualified voters choose a location for it at the first election held in the county.

This clause resulted in a controversial and bitter competition between several villages in the area, but mostly between Cedarburg, West Bend, and Port Washington. The battle for the county seat, a common phenomenon at the time all over the newly created country, took on a special contentiousness there, so much so that the state legislature, seeing no other way to solve the dilemma, got involved in 1853 and divided the county again to form Ozaukee.

Yet all of that came later, after the white man claimed the land for his own and brought his petty squabbles and his improvements. In the meantime, a very few hardy settlers were entering the land and hacking a trail that would one day bring a semblance of civilization to the wilderness. But Cedarburg did not yet exist, either in imagination or reality. First, and nearby, there was New Dublin.

2. NEW DUBLIN

Let the farmer forsake his barren hills and 'stony ground,' where he but starves to live, and lives to starve. . .

–Wisconsin Democrat, 1837

Ireland in this period was a feudal Catholic country; her people mired in a futile effort to survive that was made more difficult by repressive Protestant-English land laws and the export (to the exclusive benefit of the British, not the Irish) of the island's only cash crop—wheat. Families working the wheat fields struggled to survive on potatoes (some families eating as many as 20 pounds a day, with no meat and only scant dairy products to supplement that diet) while they harvested wealth for the British Empire. As of 1839 and 1840, the Great Irish Potato Famine would not happen for five more years, but the writing was on the wall, and dissatisfaction on the Emerald Isle reigned. Those who could emigrate to America seized the opportunity.

It was the economic pressure that pushed Irish settlers to land at a 25-foot drop in Cedar Creek along an Indian trail a mile from Cedarburg in 1839 and 1840. The settlers, in a nostalgic gesture, called their new hamlet, part of the Hamburg township and occupied by scarcely 15 residents, New Dublin after their former capital city.

They came because of the military plank road that had been torn from the forest and laid over an Indian trail running from Chicago to Green Bay. Plank roads are precisely what they sound like they are, wooden planks laid through the forest. Built initially for military purposes, they gave troops a fairly easy path from fort to fort. Plank roads soon became the rage all over the wilderness because they gave settlers a means to travel with oxen and crop-laden carts through the woods to urban centers.

"Trail Blazing" as a term enters the American vernacular at this point, as it described the notching of great cuts in the trees between which the roads would eventually be built. The trail blazing surveyors would wander the forest, chipping or "blazing" a series of trees along the Indian trails, providing the cutters, fellers, and grubbers following them with a series of easily discernable light color patches through the forest primeval.

The Green Bay Road was built mainly to facilitate troop movement between Fort Dearborn in Illinois and Fort Howard in Green Bay. It followed roughly what is now Teutonia Avenue from Milwaukee north toward Cedarburg, but turning to bypass the town to the east. The chief of the road crew decided that the spot at which the road crossed Cedar Creek was the ideal place for his permanent cabin, and so he put down a rough-hewn log house there.

The *History of Washington and Ozaukee Counties, Wisconsin* described the story this way:

> It was in 1836 and 37 that "Miserly Joe" Gardinier led a team that cut the Green Bay Road—two rods wide—along the old Indian trail which had been surveyed in 1831–32. Trees felled across water served as bridges. As nearly as can be ascertained, "Miserly Joe," was the first white man to make an onslaught and break the solid phalanx of the forests in this section. Joe was employed by the agents who had charge of the survey and construction of the old Milwaukee and Green Bay road, and made his headquarters in a little log shanty near Cedar Creek, where the Hamilton Mills now stand.

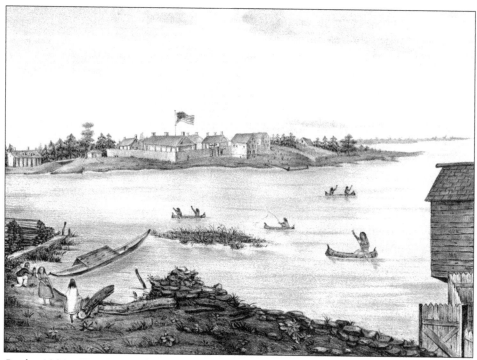

In the 1830s, Fort Howard at Green Bay was the only "civilization" north of Milwaukee. Its garrison protected white settlers and controlled the fur trade. However, the only way to get to Green Bay from Milwaukee or Chicago was by water, making the Green Bay Plank Road a necessity. (Courtesy of the Wisconsin State Historical Society.)

After the surveyors and road cutters went through the woods, a team of grubbers followed, clearing the land of stumps and brush with teams of oxen. The roadbed was chosen for its generally level nature, as there were no heavy grading machines available to the teams, but they did the best they could after tree-felling and stumping. At that point, long beams or "stringers" were imbedded in two parallel trenches as far apart as a wagon's wheels, and then across those stringers were nailed 8-foot planks. On one side of the wooden roadway, and flush with it, the ground was rolled and packed to a width of 10–12 feet to form a more or less continuous turnout track for passing.

Plank roads were seen by pioneers as better alternatives than rail because these roads of wood cost a tenth as much as did roads of rail. Farmers could also enjoy all-season travel on these relatively smooth and dry plank roads, although some farmers reported that plank roads were nearly impassable in marshy areas during the wet season. Still, the farmers who could use the roads found that their travel time to market was cut in half.

The Green Bay Road was the first major such roadway constructed in Wisconsin Territory, and the speed with which travelers could now travel was impressive. Where it had taken 30 days for mail carriers to make the trip from Chicago to Green Bay on the Indian trail, after construction of the plank road it took a mere 11 to 12 days. One traveler detailed spending two hours on the Green Bay Plank Road and covering 16 miles, while after leaving the plank it took him and his team two days to travel the remaining 24 miles to his destination.

In 1848, the state legislature chartered the Milwaukee to Fon du Lac Plank Road, which went through downtown Cedarburg and housed three toll stations, including one just south of Cedarburg, along the route. Later that year, another plank and macadam (crushed gravel) road was built from Ulao (a lakeside community, due east of Cedarburg, that had a port at the time) through Hamburg township (Grafton and Cedarburg) and on to Hartford following the route that state Highway 60 now takes. According to the Ozaukee County Historical Society's newsletter, "The roadbed consisted of a paving of wood-charcoal and burnt clay. It was supposed to have been similar to the construction of the Roman Appian Way."

Seeing the usefulness of plank roads in an otherwise unbroken wilderness, the territorial legislature chartered the Watertown Plank Road Company well before statehood, and after statehood rechartered it and 15 others. By 1853 there were 32 plank road companies building throughout the state. To make the roads pay for themselves, tolls were authorized on the road system, usually 2¢ per mile for a cart with two animals pulling.

The roads, however, later disappointed investors—tolls were too low and could not be charged by weight, only by number of beasts pulling. Scofflaws used the plank roads between the toll booths, but skirted the booths to avoid payment, and the cost of maintaining the roads was high. Additionally, the oak that was used couldn't be dried appropriately before laying, so the green oak planks rotted, a process accelerated by the changing Wisconsin seasons. These additional and

This is a gristmill like the first built in New Dublin (Hamilton) in 1839. The log and daub construction on a short stone base was inexpensive, utilitarian, and fairly sturdy. The structures had large doors on both ends of the building so that long logs could be funneled through the saws that were kept moving by waterpower.

unforeseen maintenance costs only applied further stress to an already shaky financial structure. When all was said and done, the roads simply did not pay for themselves.

Nonetheless, the enthusiastic road building continued in the 1840s and 1850s, so by the end of 1852 there were 150 miles of plank roads in Wisconsin. Five years later, there were 1,000 miles of plank, mostly within 60 miles of the port towns on the lake. And New Dublin, because of Miserly Joe, stood at the center of that road building trend.

Within feet of Miserly Joe's log shack, a group of Irish immigrants built dwellings and a sawmill, calling their district in Hamburg township (townships were large swaths of land created for political purposes) New Dublin. These men were most likely road workers or families of former road workers, since pre-famine Irish immigrants were often manual laborers instead of farmers, lacking the money to buy lands. Few whole families settled here in the rough woods since the settlement in its earliest days was the exclusive purview of men.

Ruben Wells built the area's first sawmill in 1839 on the creek where it dropped so precipitously, 25 feet in a short distance, in combination with a gristmill. It was a frame saw, common to the time and to pioneer settlements. The saw had a blade mounted in a sash and was guided by a grooved frame that would move up and down as the waterwheel spun. The board or tree would be inserted and pushed by hand lengthwise to be sawed, creating distinctive horizontal saw marks across a length of board. Because the trees found at the time were often quite old (150 years or more) and very large, they gave the settlers planks as many as 2 feet wide.

It was in New Dublin that Valentine and Harriet Hand built an inn in 1845 where travelers regularly and almost invariably stopped for food, drink, shelter, gossip, and news. That hotel also served as an excellent rendezvous for the neighboring pioneers in which they could gather, drink and eat, tell stories (as the Irish were particularly wont to do), and crack jokes. Hand sold a bourbon he called "Mine Host," making the town's tavern a welcome sight to travelers along the road since there were no spirits for tens of miles in either direction, or a half to a full day's journey.

Others came to and improved the district, adding essential businesses such as general store, a cobbler and shoemaker, a harness maker, and a smithy. One farmer, Humphrey Desmond, would have great impact on the neighboring community of Cedarburg as he was instrumental in founding the Catholic church that anchors the city's downtown, St. Francis Borgia. Thomas O'Brien bought land next door to Desmond in 1840 at Pioneer and Wauwatosa Roads. Following Desmond's and the Hands's lead, by 1843, the Irish owned the entire southern portion of what would later become Cedarburg. Yankee and Irish names dot plat maps of the time. Halpin, Malone, Place, Fox, Brown, and Strickland were some of the names associated with this place in the woods and were the first landholders responsible for making improvements in the New Dublin area.

By 1847, as more people congregated around the intersection of road and creek, it was apparent that the name of the town was becoming problematic. Due to the similarity between it and other townships, the mail of New Dublin residents often went to Dublin, Wisconsin, in Iowa County. Some even made its way overseas to Dublin, Ireland, which would have delayed its receipt by the proper party by some months. Finally, the townsfolk hit upon a singular solution.

As the tale goes, William S. Hamilton, a relative of Alexander Hamilton, stopped at New Dublin in late 1846 to water a herd of cattle he was driving north from Illinois to Green Bay. A great drinker, he enjoyed his time at Hand's hostelry and

This stone building in New Dublin (Hamilton), built in the early 1850s, housed a general store, a blacksmith shop, and several taverns over the years. It sits next to the corner on which a house of ill-repute and dance hall stood. That has since been torn down and the land left vacant.

made certain to stop there again on his return trip, sans cows and flush with cash. On that return visit, he bought beer for everyone in the house; word got out that he was doing so and a crowd gathered from nearby homes. Someone brought up the fact that their mail had recently been misdirected, so the idea of renaming the town came up while this congregation quaffed Hamilton's brew. Being that their guest was generous to a fault as well as a relative of a famous Revolutionary War hero and former federal government official, the obvious solution dawned on almost everyone simultaneously. It was therefore drunkenly determined to honor their new best friend and beneficiary, William Hamilton, along with his famous and important relative, Alexander Hamilton, by renaming the town for them both.

The proposal wasn't exactly a slam dunk, however. It actually met with considerable opposition by the civic leaders who were not in attendance or in their cups while listening to the idea. Even with this resistance, the proposal passed, and in 1847 New Dublin District was rechristened and has ever since been known as Hamilton.

Meanwhile, the area was not blossoming as a settlement. Too few farmers settled in the area to keep the saw/gristmill open and it closed in 1842. Since the Irish and Yankees were loners for the most part and didn't bring along their families, growth and permanence suffered even though the established families that did settle there certainly tried to develop a viable settlement.

The Hands sold 1.5 acres to Ernst Hersberg, who constructed a mill at the base of the fall in the creek. He built it in 1846–1847, but his business floundered due to lack of need. So around 1853, Edward and Theodore Janssen and William Gaitzsh bought the property and constructed a beautiful stone gristmill called the Concordia Mill, which still stands today.

The name was chosen to illustrate and celebrate their harmonious business relationship and the mill did prosper, although the partnership did not. The Janssens both died within a few years whereas Gaitzsh, who was serving as state treasurer in 1854, fell prey to a larcenous assistant who made off with $30,000 in state funds on Gaitzsh's watch. With a desecrated reputation, the miller returned to Hamilton where his spirit suffered, forcing him to reevaluate his life. That reassessment caused him to sell the mill to Andrew Bodendorfer, an itinerant American adventurer who had been to Australia, California, England, and Germany. Bodendorfer went broke in 1860, but the Civil War increased demand for flour and the business again flourished in 1861. The railroad's choice to lay track through Cedarburg in 1870 caused yet another decline in the fortunes of every business in Hamilton (which later became a part of the city of Cedarburg upon incorporation in 1885).

Despite all of this, Concordia Mill's name has survived 150 plus years, recalling a time of felicity, hope, and partnership. In fact, it was in Hamilton that Cedarburg's first governing body, a board of supervisors, first and best demonstrated those virtues by meeting in 1849 to lay out roads and set up school districts. The entire Hamilton district of Cedarburg remains a distinctively felicitous place to this day.

In other parts of the county, others were also settling. In what is now Port Washington, Wooster Harrison bought the first plats of land at the head of the Sauk River. A thriving settlement grew, only to dissipate in just a few years. The time for "Washington City" was not yet; its day in the sun wouldn't arrive for another decade.

Meanwhile, the ethnic future of the county, as well as that of the whole region, was portended by the arrival in October 1839 of the first Teutonic "Old Lutheran" congregation in nearby Freistadt—due west of Hamilton in the township of Mequon. This group of Lutherans from the northern Teutonic provinces of Magdeburg, Mecklenburg, and Pomerania (all now inside a recently reconstituted Germany) represented a new purpose for their emigration—escaping religious persecution in Prussia. Those Teutons, or Germans (also called "Dutch" by Americans at the time because, while they did not share a nation state in common, they did share the "Deutsch" language), came not as individuals or single families, but in whole colonies of extended families or congregations.

These pilgrims, the "Alt Lutheraners," would be only the spearhead of a larger German immigration into Wisconsin, Ozaukee County, and especially Cedarburg that would make the village the most German of any city its size in the entire country.

This 2003 photo of the Concordia Mill matches exactly photos taken of the building over the century-and-a-half of its existence. Built in 1846–1847, the mill exhibits a timeless grace and elegance to this day.

3. OF ROCK, WATER, AND GERMANS

Here in the Midwest "the American" came into existence. . . . Hardened, battered, and challenged by the land in which everything that was weak was destroyed, a new race developed [from out of the German race]: self-confident, strong, armed with an iron ability to survive. The were suspicious, self-willed, trusting only themselves and marked by an aggressive individualism and a pronounced consciousness of freedom.

–Dietmar Kuegler, scholar

In 1817, on the tricentennial anniversary of the Lutheran Reformation, King Frederick William III of Prussia proclaimed the union of the Prussian Reformed Church (Calvinist) and the Lutheran Church. Being a Calvinist and not really understanding the dogmatism and love of doctrinal hair-splitting of Lutherans, he saw little controversy in the move. Rather, he felt that by combining the two faiths into one (the Calvinist version) he would be fostering communion and community in an otherwise splintered Prussian Empire rife with political and sectional strife. "After all," he might have said in his gray-cold Deutsch tongue, "we are none of us Papists. If we cannot share political comity, let us then share in the communion of good souls and common faith." He obviously felt he was doing the correct thing. History tells us, though, that he instead made a colossal blunder.

In the couple of hundred years since the Protestant Reformation had given the Teutonic lands both Protestant churches, the only real distinction between the Lutheran and the Calvinistic Reformed Church hinged on the issue of doctrine. These were people for whom their religious practice was deadly serious business. You might recall that they had won the right to practice their form of Christianity in the most terrible war to ever be fought on German soil: the Thirty Years War.

Fought in the early to mid-seventeenth century, the war was still a strong memory to those living in early nineteenth-century Prussia due to the horrors inflicted and the reasons for the war. It began when Hapsburg Empire officials (Catholic) attempted to extend the influence of that faith into previously Protestant Bohemia (now the Czech Republic). According to Professor Gerhard Rempel of Western New England College, this is what happened:

On May 23, 1618, a year before Ferdinand was named emperor, the Bohemian leaders unceremoniously threw two imperial officials out of a window in the palace at Prague. They fell seventy feet, but escaped with their lives, either because of the intercession of the Virgin Mary, as Catholic propagandists confidently asserted, or because they landed in a dung hill, as Protestants claimed.

In any case, civil war was now inevitable and a European conflict almost certain.

The war was fought almost exclusively on German soil by Spanish, French, German, Swedish, and Austrian armies. Finally settled by the Treaty of Westphalia, the war had a lasting impact on central Europe's development and social structure akin to that of the Great Plague. Politically and in religious issues, it redrew the map; socially, it devastated the populace. The warfare decimated the countryside and the treaty gave European princes complete power over the religiosity of their subjects. The effects of that treaty made themselves felt once again 170 years later when King Frederick William III of Prussia made his bid to bind two competing and disagreeing religious faiths. Rempel again:

> The religious settlement at Westphalia confirmed the predominance of Catholicism in southern Germany and of Protestantism in northern Germany. The principle accepted by the Peace of Augsburg of 1555 that Catholic and Lutheran princes could determine the religion practiced in their territory was buttressed and strengthened, and this privilege was extended to include the Calvinists as well.
>
> [But] the real losers in the war were the German people. Over 300,000 had been killed in battle. Millions of civilians had died of malnutrition and disease, and wandering, undisciplined troops had robbed, burned, and looted almost at will. Most authorities believe that the population of the Empire dropped from about 21,000,000 to 13,500,000 between 1618 and 1648. Even if they exaggerate, the Thirty Years War remains one of the most terrible in history.

An event of such magnitude can hardly be forgotten by the ancestors of those who survived it, especially in such times when reading was a limited practice and the oral tradition was the primary form of socialization.

At the heart of the issue for Lutherans, who were asked to worship as Calvinists did, lay doctrinal differences. The act of eating bread and drinking wine during the Lord's Supper, or Holy Communion, to the Calvinists was entirely symbolic. To good Lutherans, however, that couldn't be farther from the real truth. They truly believed that the bread and wine contained the actual body of Christ, "in, with, or under" it, according to their teachings. Bridging the gap between the two camps was not going to be easy, a point Frederick William had evidently dismissed.

Yet another, and possibly more important, difference was in the two sects' understanding of predestination—the idea that all things and events in our lives are predestined by some omniscient and omnipotent being. The Lutherans, having great faith in the malleability of mankind, paid little heed to the idea and actually thought it faintly ridiculous. The Calvinists on the other hand, placing themselves totally in the hands of God, placed far greater emphasis on predestination's importance and impact on their lives. The Calvinists, a far more dour bunch, also placed a greater emphasis on developing the moral character of their flock and fostering a sincere belief in God, instead of on what they saw as the ridiculous Lutheran habit of quibbling over doctrinal questions.

And so while Frederick William's "union" of religions caused great consternation among the Lutheran communities in the north of Prussia, the Calvinists merely shrugged. But the states of Saxony, Mecklenburg, and Pomerania, where Lutherans predominated, saw the union as an attempt to uproot their very faith, the bedrock on which their existence rested.

To Lutherans who were products of a society unafraid of spilling blood over seemingly minor doctrinal differences, King Frederick William's pronouncement that they simply worship his way was a body blow not to be taken lightly. As one scholar described, "The Lutherans brought with them [to America] their own internal social disarray. From the time of the Reformation, the Lutheran

In this picture, King Frederick William III of Prussia had just assumed the throne in 1797. He ruled Prussia as a Calvinist and vehement Protestant, holding Catholic incursions into Prussia at bay until 1840.

29

reformers had produced exact, precise, and systematic doctrines." In essence, the Lutherans claimed the king wanted them to disregard the only "correct" way to worship God for an apostate's. The doctrinal difference might seem silly or petty to us today, but it most certainly was not to them.

The good King Frederick William didn't do too much to enforce his new union of faiths at first, and Lutherans all over the northern coast of Prussia ignored his edict with the determination of one who ignores a panhandler on the subway. He rightly began to see this agitation against his Calvinist approach to worship as a threat to his own rule. Since one can't have threats to one's rule running about in one's kingdom, Frederick William decided to take action.

Given that the new land of America was now open for business and gladly accepting immigrants, Frederick William decided that letting his Lutherans leave was better than clapping them in irons. So, when in 1839 several Lutheran clergy were imprisoned for resisting the union of the churches, the government began "allowing Lutherans who could prove they were part of a congregation led by a pastor, emigrat[e] en masse."

Johannes Grabau was one of those first Lutheran pastors to be imprisoned and subsequently released, with the implicit "suggestion" that he vacate the country and take his followers along. He very quickly received permission to lead a group of Alt Lutheraners to America.

Grabau was joined in Hamburg on his journey by another disaffected Prussian Lutheran, Captain Henry von Rohr, a former soldier who had lost his

In this wood cut from the period of the Thirty Years War we see a sampling of the destruction inflicted upon the Teutonic countryside, not only by armies but by roving bands of mercenaries. The famine and the disease that followed the passage of the armies made an indelible impression on all German-speaking people that would be recalled until the late nineteenth century by immigrants to America.

commission for refusing to support the union. These two gathered about them their families and congregations and did something innovative in the annals of German immigration to America—they emigrated not as individuals or single families, but as whole colonies of extended families. Many would follow their example.

The first wave, roughly 1,000 original settlers strong from the provinces of Magdeburg, Mecklenburg, and Pomerania, were led to locations already scouted out by von Rohr for the purpose. He had chosen one near Buffalo and another near Cedarburg—both being reminiscent of "Das Vaterland" in topography and geology. Of those that accompanied the pair to America, half stayed in Buffalo, New York and the other half wound up in Freistadt. The latter group, having been prosperous farmers, craftsmen, and merchants, bought nearly half of Mequon and considerable portions of Cedarburg. The congregation, consisting of over 30 families and well over 300 people, called itself Trinity and built a permanent structure in 1844.

Eventually both Grabau and Rohr made repeated recruiting trips back and forth bringing "Alt Lutherans" to Ozaukee County. A large second wave followed the Freistadters in 1843, encouraged by positive reports from the first group. These set up in Kirchayn, west of Cedarburg, becoming another sphere of influence that brought even more settlers to the town. These waves of Alt Lutherans populated the region quickly, acquiring land along the previously all-Irish Green Bay Road. More than 3,000 eventually settled in mostly Cedarburg and Freistadt.

Religious persecution, although a new element in immigration, was not the only driving factor in scattering German across the North American continent. But it was a primary reason for the creation and growth of the German element in and around Cedarburg. Richard Zeitlein of the Wisconsin State Historical Society described the reasons behind the Teutonic diaspora:

> For centuries the social system of the Germanic regions remained feudalistic and unchanging. Farmers were virtually serfs of their overlords; artisans abided by the ancient regulations of the medieval crafts guilds. So regimented was life that each type of agricultural worker, each type of artisan from each region, province, or state could be readily distinguished by his distinctive dress, made of homespun materials and dyed by hand. It was a world aptly described by the old saying, "Everybody in his place and a place for everybody."
>
> The French Revolution, with its liberating ideals, abolished this rigid system altogether and led to changes which set the stage for the eventual migrations. Agricultural reforms, industrialization, the rise of capitalism, a 38 per cent increase in the birth rate, a disastrous potato blight and other crop failures in the period between 1846 and 1853 all conspired to produce an army of dispossessed farmers. Artisans, displaced by factory workers, roamed the countryside in search of employment. To such people America did indeed seem the land of hope and shining promise.

However, the rest of the Teutonic states failed to share King Frederick William's eagerness to be rid of their Alt Lutheraners and looked with less enthusiasm upon the departure of their best and brightest.

For the most part, one could say that the German state and duchies opposed immigration on principle—remember the decimation of the German countryside in the Thirty Years War? The land and the people had not healed, even 150 years later. An official report on "Emigration from the Kingdom of Wurttenburg" reads, in part:

> The present emigration is composed chiefly of tillers of the soil, hardy and robust men whose loss from the rural districts will be much more felt than would the drawing off of a corresponding number of the population from the cities, which are comparatively over-crowded, and where the unemployed and criminal classes are generally found. . . . But those who are emigrating are the tillers in the fields and vineyards, men . . . who generally have mechanical skills as well. They compose the element we can least afford to lose.

They could thank the good King Frederick, who started the Lutheran diaspora with his blunder of 1817.

As a result of this "report," Wurttenburg required in 1837 that emigres deposit 300 florins (roughly $100 at the time and $2,000 in today's dollars) with the authorities—a sum that would be returned only upon their arrival in America. While this posed for many a deterrent, it had the happy effect of providing a sizable bankroll for those who could afford to leave it on deposit. You see, they would get it back just when they needed it most, to pay for their trip to a port of disembarkation in Europe and the ship's passage to America. If they were wise and listened to the emigres writing home with lists of supplies and provisions for the trip, their journey would already have been paid for in advance, thanks to the Wurttenburg government.

These Alt Lutheraner immigrants from the Baltic regions were economic overachievers, possessing a peculiar determination and will to succeed in their new, free environment.

They were still reserved and taciturn in the northern German way, but were also open to new experiences and to one another in their congregation and community. Said one historian in *Baltic Teutons: Pioneers of America's Frontier*, "shared language did not mean shared experience." He noted that the northern and southern Teutons differed in mood and manner:

> Northern Germans were sterner of mood, taciturn and serious. Their land made them hard working, persevering, and austere. They were cautious in assessing their [new] lands and used a formal personal approach based in tradition. Their political sectionalism and rugged individualism encouraged synodical separation of their churches.

This log barn shows us how careful the original Alt Lutheraner settlers were where their livestock was concerned. Structures like this (less the more modern shingling) were built to shelter the cattle, pigs, and horses from the frigid Wisconsin winters, and with all the animal body heat contained, they were quite snug.

These characteristics made Alt Lutheraners able to fend for themselves in virgin land, whether it was in isolation or in the company of neighbors. Hard workers all of them, these Teutons were unafraid to tame land an acre at a time, carefully growing the extent of their lands through clearing a handful of acres a year. The usual goal was clearing 40 acres per year, something done in the winter. This not only provided them with ample building material at first, but also heating and cooking, as well as fuel for steam shipping if they could get it to a dock. However, most of that felled lumber went up in smoke, since fire was often the only way to get rid of it. As Zeitlin puts it:

> One important attitude which German settlers displayed in Wisconsin was a feeling of proprietorship towards their new land. Conditioned by European memories, they looked on the land as the foundation, the basis for an estate that could be passed on to succeeding generations, a viewpoint that assigned locational stability. Many Yankees, on the other hand, thought of their land as a resource to be exploited, to be used for speculation, and perhaps to be sold. "They did not give back to the soil those elements necessary to maintain its fertility," observed a Washington County historian in comparing Yankee and German

33

farmers. "For this reason Wisconsin was fortunate to be favored so much by the German immigrant farmer who came here to stay. . ."

Moreover, according to Reverend A. F. Evast, writing in 1889, German farmers taught Americans methods of "rational farming," by rotating crops and the liberal use of fertilizer—a practice summarized in the old German folk sayings, "The manure pit is the farmer's gold pit." and "Where there is manure there is Christ." Above all, the German farmer eschewed speculation, preferring to invest his savings in neighboring fields with which he was intimately familiar. Avoiding risks and adventurous experiments necessitating loans, Germans were content to cultivate their small plots intensively, and to progress slowly but steadily towards stability and success.

Caring for livestock [also] seems to have been related to German attitudes towards sound farming practices. Settlers who arrived with enough capital soon constructed barns to house their livestock. Johann Kerler expressed the general feeling when he wrote in 1849: "I could not bring myself to leave cattle out in the open during the cold months as the milk would freeze in the cow's udder."

This log cabin and outbuilding were the type of shelter thrown up by those first settlers in Freistadt. They used the ample supply of felled logs and made a daub from the limestone they crushed to fill the gaps between logs. This quickly-built housing protected them from the fierce Wisconsin winters.

And so while Yankees tended to seek out prairie lands from which they could develop a quick profit and then move on, the German-speaking people operated from the long view, initially eking out survival in the woods. They planned ahead, cared for, and nurtured into being a fully developed farm to deed to their children. That approach resulted in creating cultivated farmland from a place so heavily forested in 1831 that one surveyor noted, "A squirrel could probably make it's [sic] way from Green Bay to Chicago and never touch the ground." Keeping an eye on their progeny's well-being is manifested today in Cedarburg's stone and brick structures.

But the primary attribute developed by the German frontiersman, as noted by the famed western frontier professor Frederick Jackson Turner, was that of being "on guard" as they experienced strange foods, foreign lands, and curious people, making the Germans supremely respectful of the dangers that accompanied those phenomena. This, in turn, engendered a deep respect for difference and diversity, not to mention a caution and sensitivity to changing environmental factors.

From a frontier letter to family in Germany by Gerhard Kremers of Newton, Wisconsin, a village some miles north of Sheboygan and only 30 miles from Cedarburg, we get a sense of what it meant to be "on guard:"

> Now a word about the Indians. These have been described so often that I might omit writing about them. I may state, however, the first time an immigrant meets them in the woods they make an unfavorable impression. For the most part they are armed with rifle and bow, live exclusively from hunting and fishing, and roam from one place to another. They are said to be particularly skilled in shooting. Wherever they go they erect their tents and lead a lazy life. It is only by seeing them repeatedly that one gets used to them. We are by this time, since groups of 10–30 frequently pass by, mostly on horseback. Occasionally, they ask for a drink of water or a pipe of tobacco. One need not fear them. No longer have they any claim to the land . . . their number is not great.

Kremers continued his advice after he had put minds at ease about the "lazy" and less than savage natives. Immigrants who expect to board themselves on the ship's journey to America "should provide themselves with dried fruits, dried beef, ham, Rollfleisch [beef prepared like sausage and cooked and pickled in vinegar]. In addition Zweiback, with fresh cabbage and Sauerkraut, vinegar, herring, and also a few apples." He also suggested wooden shoes to warm the feet (which will always be wet, he warned), and they "will want leather soles or they'll slip on the wet decks."

Also contained in his rather long list for newcomers were feather beds ("not to be found anywhere here"), flatirons, coffee mills, cord and ropes, carpenter tools, and other milled and/or iron tools like spades and shovelheads.

It was this type of letter, and hundreds of others like it, that convinced the German people to come to America to try their fortunes. In Germany at the time, "reading groups" gathered regularly to read and discuss literature; by 1840, the main material of these groups were letters from friends and acquaintances who had moved to Wisconsin or Buffalo, New York. Simply put, the reaction of the governments in Europe was reactionary. Already in 1820, Prussia had made emigration altogether illegal, but due to the letters from America encouraging exodus there, the Prussian authorities in 1845 made a law that prohibited reading in public any letter or paper which might, even indirectly, encourage emigration.

That law and the others designed to keep the sieve that was Teutonic society from leaking German-speaking people all over another continent failed. More and more people like Christian Groth heard from Teutons about the fair lands in the area around Cedarburg and in America generally. He determined to accompany his fellow Alt Lutheraners and sent his sons in 1842, hoping to follow later.

And so it was that four of the six Groth brothers came to America in 1842: Johann, Martin, Ferdinand Ludwig, and Wilhelm. They and their father had been landowners in Treptow, and immediately bought 120 acres of land in Cedarburg for $925 ($7.71 per acre) from George Warren, who originally purchased it in 1840 for $1.25. Conditions facing the Groths were primitive almost beyond imagination. First they built a stick shelter on the site of the present winery (more to keep animals out than weather). Later they cut logs to build a small two-room structure that had one small window with a wood closure in each room. These primitive homes gave way to taller ones with warm lofts where the children would sleep, and eventually two-story log houses, in the 1850s.

They purchased more land around that original stake and set aside some land for a small village along the creek. F. Ludwig Groth, who must have been the real visionary of the four, planned a thriving village in the center of the land through which Cedar Creek "rollicks along moraines of scenic Niagra [sic] limestone rock formations," and spills out into the Milwaukee River a couple miles downstream. Thus, his selection of the site for a town can be summed up in one word—waterpower.

In Groth's time the steam engine had not yet been perfected and water, animal, or wind drove all large mills and industrial works. Every small community had some sort of mill, although if no water source was available the gears were turned by beast or breeze. The free waterpower was harnessed for a variety of purposes, but in pioneer America it was used mainly to saw wood for building or grind grain for use and sale. Groth could see that Cedar Creek had a virtually unlimited supply and source of waterpower to drive mills, all due to that 1.5 mile stretch in Cedarburg where the creek descends 80 feet. History proved him right; within a few decades of his arrival, the creek boasted five dams operating five mills to grind wheat (mostly as a cash crop) and barley, oats, corn, and rye for woolen products or finishing wood (sawing and planing, manufacturing of moldings, etc.).

Another piece of the Cedarburg equation, the area's limestone, evidenced itself when he built a limestone house from stone quarried from the lot he owned. It stands on the corner of what is now Evergreen and Western, and was later sold to

This plat map shows the Groth holdings in early Cedarburg. F. Ludwig Groth envisioned a village along Cedar Creek and made sure to parcel out the land in his control carefully to those who would build businesses and settle permanently. (From the Rappold Collection.)

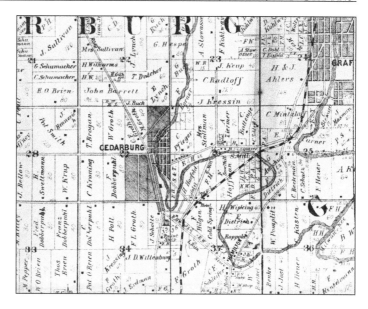

Carl Dobberpuhl and remained in that family until quite recently, when another Dobberpuhl bought it and then vacated it in the late twentieth century.

Carl Dobberpuhl was only one of many Alt Lutherans from in and around Treptow to follow the Groths to Cedarburg. Hugo Pool, Thomas Brokow, and Dr. Fred Luening and their families made the trip in 1843 with the rest of their Treptow congregation. At the same time as the sale of that stone house, the pair (Groth and Dobberpuhl) gave the adjacent land to their congregation's place of worship, Trinity Church, for use as a place of devotion and as a cemetery (now called Founders Park). The group found that the limestone lay so close to the surface in the cemetery that it would take two men two days to blast a grave deep enough to bury a body. The work was so time consuming, expensive, and dangerous that the church decided to find a new cemetery, buying the land for Zur Ruhe across the creek.

Conditions in no way matched any of the experiences these Europeans had in their homeland. Dangers abounded, especially the wildlife, which gave the settlers quite a few scares. They were very few people in a vast forest wilderness and very self-conscious of that fact. To be frightfully respectful of the wolves that came around to the shelters or on long hikes to Milwaukee carried no shame. They also feared the Native Americans, and had heard a story that they had taken a disliking to a Saukville man, killed him and his wife and took their daughter for themselves. As the tale goes, the man's brother saved the daughter and the pair made their way to safety in Washington City. The isolated incident only increased settlers' unease.

Scattered bands of natives continued to live near Green Bay Road while traders, soldiers, settlers, and mail carriers used the road heavily. The largest village sat where Interstate 43 now runs near the Milwaukee River, with another scattered population living along the creek and north of town near the bog. They

These Native Americans carrying pails of maple syrup showed the Teutonic farmer/settlers of Cedarburg how to tap the abundant sugar maple trees for the sap and to boil it down to extract sugar. Maple sugar was the sweetener used by pioneer women to flavor cookies and cakes for decades. (Courtesy of the Wisconsin State Historical Society.)

demonstrated genuine friendliness to the newcomers by teaching the Groths and others how to harvest maple syrup and boil it down for sugar.

The first settlers in Cedarburg picked the wild raspberries, strawberries, and blackberries that were quite plentiful. They tripped over the butternuts and hickory nuts that grew liberally and wild all around them. They hunted deer, wolves, mink, raccoons, skunks, and squirrels in the old Indian hunting grounds. Game birds also flourished in the area, especially the passenger pigeon. So many would congregate that tree limbs would snap off under their weight and settlers quickly learned they could net the birds, gathering enough to feast for days and still take the remainder into Milwaukee for sale.

The holdings of Ludwig Groth eventually included all of north Cedarburg; everything above the interurban tracks to Bridge Street and from Third Street to Jefferson Avenue was his, according to a plat he recorded in 1844. He turned out to be something of a speculator and real estate developer, although it appears he sometimes bought and sold on a whim or inkling. He divided a large section of his land in the heart of Cedarburg into 71 lots, filing a plat with the land office on December 1, 1844, and started his real estate career with sales to Charles Dettmering and Jacob Lange two weeks later. He sold some of the small plots, 3–5 acres, for $5–10 an acre. He later sold eight lots for a total of $22.80, then another one for $6, making several hundred percent profit. He must have felt like he was making money hand over fist, but to another speculator it would have seemed like nothing compared to where the prices might head if the town became a going concern. And become a going concern Cedarburg did, especially after Frederick Hilgen and William Schroeder came to town.

4. FATHER HILGEN AND COMPANY

The German families come with bags of gold, some of them have $20,000 and upwards . . . They are hardy and intelligent, and will be a great acquisition to the wealth and industry of the country.

–Milwaukee Sentinel, September 10, 1839

Cedarburg looked in 1844 like countless other hardscrabble frontier settlements in the American West: a set of dirt tracks running through dense forests to scattered log buildings sitting amidst stump-littered fields growing with golden wheat. Little evidence of civilization spoiled the mostly pristine wilderness, no permanent structures jostled the woodlands. No schools, mills, or even homes made of anything but log and daub could be seen in the area. The landscape, that which could be seen in the few clearings, bespoke its rough-hewn frontier beginning.

That unimproved forest would have been the vision that evidenced itself as Frederick Hilgen arrived in Cedarburg on a scouting trip with his close friend and business partner William Schroeder. Hilgen saw the forest's future even through the trees, envisioning a teeming city by the creek with mills, shops and townspeople prospering. Hilgen also brought more than just the vision—he brought a bag of gold. That financing, in conjunction with his native intellect and industry, would be what was needed to found the permanent community that would become Cedarburg.

This pair of German explorers and merchants, prosperous business partners in Charleston, South Carolina, had deep family and friendly connections in Kirchhatten, Oldenburg in northern Germany. They not only saw what the Groth family witnessed when they arrived in town, but they also had a way of financing their goals.

Confident he could find the financing to transform the wilderness, Hilgen once wrote to his brother-in-law and main financier, C. Frederick Boerner, "I think this will be a prosperous town." Boerner would loan Hilgen and Schroeder many thousands of dollars in the coming years, and all at half the going rate. Boerner's money (his store in Charleston was very prosperous and, using the profits from it, he functioned as a private banker both there and for gold prospectors on their way to California) and the cash Hilgen and Schroeder generated from their milling businesses would be more than sufficient for their needs. Hilgen became the driving force behind the building of a prosperous Cedarburg and he would be primarily responsible for marshalling the financial investments that would make it a reality. He became a one-man industrial revolution, the town's Chief Executive Officer, its chamber of commerce, and the village's chief social director all wrapped into one. His personality, both fun-loving and forceful, and his drive to make Cedarburg an island of teutonic prosperity amidst the forests of southeastern Wisconsin would result in his being reverently and lovingly called by townsfolk "Father" Hilgen to this very day.

Frederick Hilgen began his life in America in the large German-speaking colony of Charleston, South Carolina. He was ambitious and hardworking, trained at farming, but also having had exposure to politics and community involvement through his father, who was "Untervogt," or a sub-governor, bailiff, or under-sheriff in the homeland. You could say an Untervogt was almost an official henchman, according to historical accounts, and was the "muscle" teutonic princes used to find, arrest, and punish evil-doers, or at least those who disagreed with the crown.

The city from which Hilgen came to America, a small dorf named Kirchhatten in a tiny duchy named Oldenburg, is now over 1,100 years old and built on the side of a moor. Because of the chill and the damp, not to mention a dearth of trees, many permanent buildings were built with stone quarried from several hundred miles away.

Born on April 3, 1805, Hilgen learned farming as a youth from his father, but upon arrival in America in 1832, he took up the grocery trade, working for a general store and grocer in the Charleston "Dutch," or German-speaking community in that "rambunctious and vibrant port city built on mud and logs loaded with cobblestone ballast, where the harbor was protected by seawalls of crushed oyster shells." At the time, and until today, "Charleston's leading citizens were of English or Scottish ancestry, and made up a select and small society" which other ethnicities of language groups could not hope to permeate. Still, Germans poured into the new country's premier southern Atlantic seaport in droves to develop new lives.

Hilgen worked hard and well, and in just two years he ended up owning his own grocery along with William Schroeder, who remains something of a cipher. From his constant presence in the shadows, though, he seemed to be the consummate "shopkeeper" who was conscientious, careful, conservative and pleasant. Becoming Cedarburg's first postmaster from 1847 to 1853 proves that he was trusted by all.

Schroeder came from Kirchhatten as well and had friends and family among the Oldenburgers. He appears to have been connected to Hilgen from the time he was a young adult in almost every business venture, but what is missing from the record is his exact relationship with Hilgen. The maiden name of Hilgen's mother,

Scenes like these played out over and over again in port cities like Charleston, South Carolina, where Frederick Hilgen and C. Frederick Boerner began their American lives. People by the tens of thousands disembarked in the seaports, seeking a new life in the New World. Likewise, getting to their final destination in America often meant traveling again by boat only to disembark. This depiction, c. 1850, shows the Milwaukee River. (Courtesy of the Wisconsin State Historical Society.)

Anna-Maria, was Schroeder and it can be supposed that William Schroeder was at least a cousin to Hilgen.

By way of conjecture it can also be said that Schroeder played second fiddle to Hilgen's concertmaster since all the businesses they created carried Hilgen's name, first or solely, while Schroeder was always left "minding the store." Whatever the precise familial relationship between the two, they enjoyed an excellent working relationship. They would be involved together in countless business ventures between 1834 and Hilgen's death in 1878.

Together the men owned a store in the bustling seaside trading and shipping town of Charleston for almost eight years, prospering and developing a close business relationship with another store keeper from Oldenburg and future Cedarburg resident, Christoph Frederick Boerner. These three, plus Frederick Behrens, soon also to be of Cedarburg, belonged to the same all-German paramilitary group, the German Fusilier Society. The Charleston colonists created the Fusiliers in 1775 to act as a militia in defense of the colony's efforts at independence and functioned as a kind of reserve militia right up to and through the Civil War. Hilgen, alone of the four, saw duty with the Fusiliers in the Florida Everglades during the Seminole Indian War—while Schroeder minded the store.

Hilgen felt prosperous enough after two years as a merchant to return home to Kirchhatten in 1837 to marry. In the tribal marriage pattern of the Alt Lutheraners, he married his close friend Boerner's sister Louise, returning with her to their Charleston home and business. And so the "Charleston Group" of Hilgen, Schroeder, and Boerner lived and prospered for six more years in the deep South. But Hilgen soured on the town's climate after Louise lost four of her five babies. The family tradition has it that Hilgen blamed Charleston's heat and humidity for their singular tragedy, the result of which was Cedarburg's particular gain.

Casting about for locations where he could raise a healthy family, Hilgen and Schroeder caught wind of the then thriving city of Milwaukee, Wisconsin. Milwaukee in those years drew German-speakers like iron filings to a magnet. The city was bursting with growth; in 1840, the city had 1,700 residents; in 1843, it had over 6,000. The construction noise was remarkable in itself, according to one account, and a *Milwaukee Sentinel*'s correspondent on August 19, 1843 commented, "I never saw so much building going on in my life. They are building houses and stores in all directions. Being here is just like living in a *carpenter's shop*—the sound of hammers heard continuously." Hilgen and Schroeder sold their shops and

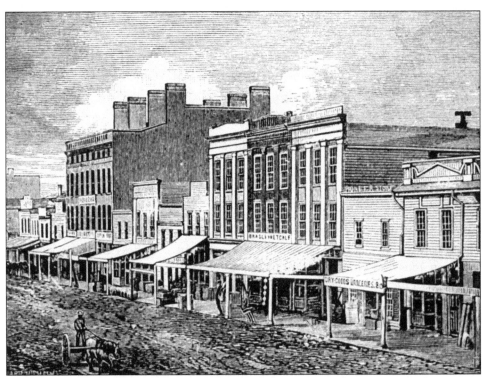

This line of newly built storefronts could as easily be from 1843 Charleston as 1843 Milwaukee or 1843 Chicago. It happens to be Milwaukee in that year; the location of Hilgen and Schroeder's first Wisconsin store was right around the corner from this view of downtown. (Courtesy of the Wisconsin State Historical Society.)

moved in 1843, buying a store together in Milwaukee's downtown at 217 East Water Street.

Sometime in 1843, Hilgen and Schroeder made a trip up the Green Bay Road to Cedarburg. Hilgen was 38, in the prime of his life, and, as he later wrote to a friend, knew immediately that this spot on a creek was the place he would set down roots. He would bring his family "to a place that was just beginning to come alive."

When Hilgen purchased his original Cedarburg stake of 160 acres for $800 from Charles Melms on April 13, 1844, he had just turned 39. He eventually bought over 400 acres, selling some of it off in speculation. But Hilgen knew that any vital community needed a mill to create prosperity. Jerry Apps and Allan Strang write, in their *Mills of Wisconsin,* that mills were not only the first factories in every frontier town, presaging the industrial revolution, but along with church and school, were considered as key to a community's health.

Often, they write, a mill was the community's absolute center, at least in the beginning before there were churches or schools. It also functioned as the focal social spot, a place where farmers met and talked while their grains were milled, or where the town would meet on important issues. Write Apps and Strang:

> The mill was the club. Here the henpecked and the wife beaters could all meet and relieve their minds and regain their self-respect if it was tottering. Here the local statesmen and the religious ranters could find an audience. Here the farmer could ascertain how his neighbors' crops were coming on in the drought, what chances there was of a schoolmaster being found . . .

Hilgen and Schroeder began building a saw and gristmill on land they felt would become their town center. They also found it prudent to cut a road to Green Bay Road (Hamilton Road) from the mill so farmers would not have to cross the creek on their trip. They felt these moves would encourage people to settle in Cedarburg near their mill (and on the west side of the creek) because of the easy access.

They finished the mill in 1845, just before a Dr. Luening built his Columbia Mill to serve the farmers on the east side of the creek. Luening, however, in building his mill also built a dam that flooded 5 acres of Hilgen land. In this incident and its aftermath we see the power of community opinion in a small frontier town and also get an inkling of how strictly these Germans adhered to the idea of developing the commonwealth. Hilgen attempted several times to convince Luening to destroy or modify his dam, until in 1847 he felt compelled to sue. The conflict between business rivals continued until 1850. At one point Luening and his co-defendant Joseph Yenkel faced Judge Charles Larrabee's wrath because they failed to appear in court for a hearing when Luening claimed was too ill to make the trip. He finally made an appearance before the judge and had the trial moved to Dodge County where he hoped he would get a fair hearing, since public opinion around Cedarburg and the vicinity was solidly in Hilgen's

Columbia Mill served farmers on the east side of the creek and was built at the same time as was Hilgen's first mill. The milldam flooded Hilgen's property, and a lawsuit ensued and dragged on for years with the builder of Columbia Mill, finally leaving Cedarburg in shame. (Postcard courtesy of the Robert Armbruster Archive.)

favor. He was held liable, lost the case, and was ordered to destroy the dam as well as pay for monetary damages. Luening was sorely embarrassed, quickly selling out and leaving town in disgrace.

Businesses began to congregate in the immediate area of Hilgen's mill. Gottlie Henning set up a shoe shop in the village in 1845. In 1846, Joe Carley cleared the land at Washington Avenue and Western Avenue to build a blacksmith business where he used charcoal he made himself to start shoeing horses and creating other needed iron products. Fred Schliefer also started a shoe repair shop, and hired J.P. Wirth, a Bavarian immigrant, when Wirth arrived in Cedarburg in 1846. Wirth would ply the shoe trade with Schliefer for some years until, in 1865, he would form a partnership with his son Charles and build what would become the largest general department store in the county, called Wirths'.

At the same time they built a mill and sliced a path through the forest, Hilgen and Schroeder both built log houses in preparation for the arrival of families in 1845. The climate and the lifestyle would agree with them all; after a number of disastrous pregnancies in the swamps of the South, Louise finally gave birth to a healthy child, Johann Friederick, in the winter of 1846 in their log house. The children kept coming as a final tally would reach 13, and all nine born in Cedarburg would live to maturity. Hilgen's commercial projects prospered too.

By 1846 the town already boasted a flourmill, a sawmill, a general store, a hotel, an apothecary, a doctor, and three small log houses. The rest of the populace lived above or behind their shops.

Hilgen joined Milwaukee's Wisconsin Guards, a paramilitary force of Germans dedicated to protecting the frontier, similar to the German Fusilier Society. It is told by Alice Schimmelpfennig Wendt, the author of *Hilgen Heirs,*that the Guards "thrilled to perfection in drill and marching, building a hall in which to do so, as well as throwing banquets and dinners on political and secular holidays."

Wendt called Hilgen irrepressible, having a strong zest for life and a strong faith in the future, as was amply evidenced by the number of mills he planned, farms he built, the large amounts of money he borrowed, the vast tracts of land he bought, and the whole industries he created. He built with a grand dream of Teutonic security and prosperity.

That grand dream manifested itself in his and Schroeder's purchase of large blocks of land on behalf of their Charleston/Oldenburg friend, C. Frederick Boerner. As Hilgen finished his dam for the mill in 1846, he and Schroeder bought land for themselves and for Boerner. The three bought 67 acres of land west of the creek and north of the mill in 1847 for $2,500, locking up the water rights. They also bought, along with George Fischer and Joseph Carley, most of what was Section 27 of the township, platting it into lots and selling them quickly. That purchase and plat was called the Hilgen, Schroeder, and Others Addition. Hilgen and Schroeder also bought land to parcel out called the Hilgen and Schroeder Addition.

A letter about the town's July 4, 1846 celebration shows Hilgen in the light of civic promoter and social director. He described the day to his brother-in-law Boerner thus:

> The 4th of July was celebrated here. We started at 4 o'clock in the morning and continued until 2 at night. We had a beautiful parade, four musicians, one drummer, one with a fife, two with clarinets. When that was finished we had a speech in German and English. Then it rained hard. When that was all over, we started to dance. The dance floor was laid out behind my house under the trees. There were about 200 people. If it had not rained 500 would have come.

At the time, the entire population of Washington County wasn't much more than 1,500.

Boerner made a visit to Cedarburg later in 1846 and fell in love with the land and its potential, as Hilgen had promised. Boerner, who had a hugely prosperous business in a thriving and cosmopolitan southern seaport city, became quickly convinced that Cedarburg was the perfect place to raise a family. Here the trio could create a community of their own choosing, one where they and their families could live and prosper through the German ethos of hard work and skillful enterprise.

This portrait hangs in Klug's Creekside Inn, a restaurant inhabiting the feed store Father Hilgen and William Schroeder built across the street from their mill. Father Hilgen acted as a one-man chamber of commerce and entrepreneurial society in Cedarburg's beginnings.

A son of Boerner's, Theodore, wrote a biography of the man in 1937 in which he described Boerner's rise to wealth and prominence. The main ingredient seemed to be the fact that C. Frederick was one of the "Gemeinde Hatten," as recorded by his pastor, Reverend H. Lobeken, in 1894. In other words, namely English, Boerner was intimately connected to the Hatten congregation.

Tracking the close familial relations between these Alt Lutheraners becomes challenging because they practiced endogamy, or inter-familial marriage, within what they considered their "racial group," the Prussian or Teutonic peoples. Christoph Frederick Boerner was born in 1812, two years before his younger sister and future Mrs. Hilgen, Catharina Louise. His half brother, Frederick Christian Boerner, dealt in slaves in Charleston, which ended in disaster. F. Christian would later move to Cedarburg to join his brother and open a store. However, he left several years later for Belleville, Illinois, citing health reasons.

C. Frederick arrived in Charleston after Hilgen and Schroeder in 1837, and dropped the Christoph from his name to avoid confusion with his brother

Christian. He showed great resilience when a great fire in Charleston destroyed much of the city and two of his general stores, and unphased, he promptly rebuilt. All in all, Boerner would spend a dozen profitable years in Charleston before joining the "Charleston Group" in the idylls of Cedarburg.

He visited the town in 1846 and was enthusiastic about its potential, so he traveled to Germany to recruit immigrants for Cedarburg in 1848 even before he himself made the move there. One recruit, his cousin F. Roebken, sent a letter to Boerner apologizing for not making the move, but promising that he would "surely be in Cedarburg by next fall." Another family who knew the Boerners and Hilgens, the Vosteens, did make the trip in 1848. While traveling, Boerner left the business with his partner Juergen Schroeder (no relation to William Schroeder), a man Theodore Boerner wrote was of such high integrity that his faithful stewardship of Boerner affairs received favorable comment inside family circles long after the "Charleston Group" was dead.

Frederick Boerner married Helena Wilhelmina Hussmann in 1844 in Charleston and they would eventually bear seven children, all but one of whom died as young children. Helena herself died in 1858. Boerner then married Anna Gesina Vosteen (a new Cedarburg resident) in 1859, and proceeded to have nine more

The creek that generated enough water power to fuel five mills is shown here in a winter scene at a rapids. Frederick Boerner and Frederick Hilgen knew that this source of power could make them prosperous and secure in the wilderness. They invested their time, money, and energies to making it so.

Teutonic women of the era emigrated along with their men, carrying on the household tasks and marrying into the families that accompanied their spouses on the trek to America. These summer kitchens and outdoor cauldrons, joint ventures many of them, were the focal point of the women's work and social lives as mills were to the men's.

children, seven of whom appear to have lived to adulthood. Popular wisdom said that by the turn of the century everyone in Cedarburg was related to everyone else in Cedarburg, the result of the habit of family and business intermarriage. In this way Cedarburg exemplified the larger trend in Teutonic immigration to America, with its many Alt Lutheraner congregations (extended families all) moving there. Linda Schelbitzki Pickle in her book *Contented Among Strangers* writes that families played a central role to German immigrants. Entire extended families came together and supported one another in the process, whereas the Yankees sent their men to claim a beachhead and, in the Anglo-Saxon tradition, sent later for their women when things were stabilized in the new land. Germans, on the other hand, brought their women with them to help create a community from wilderness.

On Louise Hilgen's and Helena Boerner's place in the New World, and for all German women at the time, Pickle says, "Their [women's] traditional roles as conservators of tradition and rural family values made women central players in the immigrants group's adaptation to America." They were not, as other historians would have it, victims of the "second barrier" to immigration, one of language. The fact that they spoke no English actually benefitted them because of their Teutonic tradition and home-centered, family-focused lives. Because they spoke only German and lived among only those who did, they had an extra buffer shielding them from the jarring and traumatic experiences of cultural alienation in a New World. "European culture prepared many immigrant women to make vital contributions to frontier adaptation with less alienation than many Anglo-American women felt," Pickle writes.

Clusters of immigrants by blood, marriage, or acquaintance were typical. Whole families and congregations of churches and neighborhoods from their province or state moved to one area; Cedarburg was just such a place. Economic motivation for relocation placed a distant second to religious, philosophical, and political goals—these were fierce individualists, intensely free men. Additionally, Pickle and others assert, the charismatic leadership in such philosophic/religious settlements (as personified by the "Alt Lutherans" in general but specifically so in Kirchayn and Freistadt) marshaled the survival skills of the community more successfully than the leaders of loosely organized, cooperative groups like the Yankees or even the Teutonic emigration societies, like Dreissiger, which attempted to make Texas a "German" state.

Teutonic women enjoyed few rights, and after 1871 and the creation of the German State those became even fewer. Women could own but not administer property and essentially were wards or guardians of their husbands' estates. The Teutonic tradition of self-sacrifice and hard work, coupled with the slower pace of industrialization in Germany, meant that these women's education lagged behind the British or French. However, the Teuton women took great pride in their frontier contributions, a very different reaction than their Yankee counterparts. Daily experiences of the women proved that they made an invaluable contribution to the success of their pioneer families immediately after landing in America.

With this arrival, the attitudes of German speakers did not change. These immigrants wanted many aspects of their lives to change, in particular their freedom to worship and to own and use their land as they liked, but they didn't come to America to change the way the genders interacted in the public or the private sphere. If anything, those ideas of appropriate gender roles hardened under the stresses of surviving in a new and wholly unique setting. Still, although it was a man's world, the women "ruled the roost." One Teutonic joke from the time has it thus:

> Question: "Who advances fastest?"
> Answer: "Women. Scarcely is the courtship over and they already are
> corporals and soon they have command."

German frontier women took responsibility for acquiring, raising, procuring, preparing, and storing food. They spun the thread and wove the cloth to make the family's clothing. They provided most of the care for children and oversaw their contributions to the family labor. Rural women took charge of the livestock and dairy products (eggs, milk, and butter), did the gardening, and at peak times they were called into the fields. They also kept and nurtured the family and community's traditions, their family's communion with others, and maintained a sense of ritual as "keepers" of the Teutonic cultural and social "flame."

The hardships endured by these hardy German frontierswomen are many and varied. For example, they carried water for the household, one of the heaviest chores along with transporting wood for fires (sometimes a cord or more a day, as the stoves also heated the primitive, non-insulated homes).

For these women and their partners, birth and death were inextricably linked in pioneer society; many women died in childbirth and certainly infant mortality was extraordinarily high by our standards. Because it is hardly comprehensive, the following list from a variety of sources serves to demonstrate the tremendous toll childbirth could wreak on frontier life. So many women and infants dying while birthing in such a small population caused great sadness and disruption in the pioneers' lives.

In Cedarburg, Helen Spuhl died birthing twins in 1848 and only one of the babies survived. Dorothea Pantzloff gave birth to twins and they both died. Wilhelmine Groth (nee Dobberpuhl) gave birth ten times before dying herself from the eleventh. Her husband Ferdinand remarried to a woman named Caroline and she died a year and a quarter after Wilhelmine when giving birth to a son. Justine Liesenberg died in 1862 days after delivering a daughter. Her husband William was away serving in the Civil War at the time. As you can see, the frontier community was built on a foundation of gravestones.

Hilgen and Schroeder bought and cleared land for Boerner in preparation for his arrival, and when he did get to Cedarburg, he found an almost nearly completed farm. Boerner never stopped recruiting from or communicating with the old elements at home. A cousin of his, A. Pueschelburger, wrote Boerner often from Hatten, discussing the failures of the German Liberal movement of the 1840s and 1850s, explaining to Boerner how it affected his friends and comrades in Oldenburg.

According to his biographer, son Theodore, the attitude of the German farmers was best summed up by former Charleston resident Frederick Behrens, who told Theodore as a youth, "A farmer is best off when in debt, he has something to work for." Behrens, at least, followed the rule. Whenever he paid off his debt on a farm he bought another next to it. It would seem that many of the Boerner acquaintances followed it as well; certainly "Father" Hilgen applied the rule to industry, borrowing many tens of thousands of dollars to start new ventures as soon as the old stabilized.

The biography gives a glimpse into a way of life now long gone and never to be seen again, and Theodore Boerner relates how he watched his father sow seeds between the stumps from a pan at his side, and in an attempt to do the same was corrected by his father, who said, "Dass der wind es night fort blaset," (that the wind does not blow it away). Another childhood memory of Boerner's was listening to elders' tales of skies blackened by great flocks of passenger pigeons:

> One story [he heard often] told of a forest giant loaded down with passenger pigeons and of how the tree was chopped down and all the families round about shared in a great pigeon feast. I wondered then, and do now, why the pigeons, having wings to fly, did not fly away when the tree was cut down.

Evidently, Boerner never thought of netting, but several accounts of the period point out that the pigeons were plentiful and stupid. They were gathered like fish in nets.

Whatever he thought or he neglected to consider, Theodore Boerner points out to us with these stories that the wilderness stood close by, so close that Theodore's grandfather Vosteen once shot a deer on the road from his front porch.

None of this primitivism disturbed C. Frederick Boerner, or any of the sophisticated and cosmopolitan "Charleston Group." Rather, the wilderness invigorated these men and their families and they saw vast potential in the land they cleared and in the waterpower of the creek. They saw great opportunity for carving out from the forest their version of paradise. All it would take would be more families, more Teutonic manpower. In that regard their prayers were answered, as the coming years proved exhilaratingly expansive. All was right and as it should be in the village on the creek.

This plaque shows the names of those men and women buried in Founders Park. The vast majority of those buried were women, children, and infants, underscoring the difficulty of life in the wilderness.

51

5. From Forest,
a Teutonic Village

. . . they had their cares and troubles as they faced the hard tasks of establishing their homes and families in this new land. There was no one to solve their problems. They had to do it alone.
  –Excerpt from the Groth family history

Gristmills would be key to solving those initial problems, as Hilgen and Schroeder recognized in 1845 before they began building one. They knew that once gristmills existed along the creek, the few farmers in the area could sell crops they wrested from the newly cleared and stump-ridden woodlands, creating a surplus to help buy more land, bring more family to town, and become more prosperous. Yet security and true prosperity for families was solid and stable governmental structures that could efficiently provide services at a local level, something still lacking in the wilderness of Wisconsin Territory.

Another hurdle standing in the way of progress was reliable transportation to a port for those cash crops. The creek, for all its worth as a power source, in fact because of its worth as such, was useless as water transportation for grain shipments from Cedarburg. The shallow Milwaukee River also could not act as an appropriate road for grain shipments, or any other kind of travel for that matter. And while the Green Bay plank road lay nearby, giving farmers some access to market in Milwaukee (rapidly shaping up as the premier port city in Wisconsin), getting to the road made the trip long and often difficult, especially in bad weather.

Hilgen, in his inimitable way, set his mind to actively solving those problems. He knew he must continue gathering around his mill a large enough congregation of people to make a village, but more importantly, he needed people who could make it complete in the Teutonic sense. That first problem would solve itself through sheer inertia, freeing him to look for the particular kinds of men he needed. He knew the families and friends of the original settlers would eagerly reunite with their comrades so they could worship as they liked and live as free men.

In *The Americanization of German Immigrants: Language, Religion, and Schools in Nineteenth Century Wisconsin*, Susan Jean Kuyper's doctoral thesis from 1980, it is written:

To many Germans, the ideal was to have clustered around his farm many others owned by relatives and close acquaintances. To take complete possession of a town-ship with sons, sons-in-law, and nephews was not an unrealizable ideal. This played out in many rural locations. . .

The latter issue of finding those certain kinds of people, however, posed a stickier problem of recruitment for Hilgen, as it required a mix of serendipity and friendly coercion. The most important characteristic in those he sought was fluency in the German language, since he knew that few of the Alt Lutherans coming to this new land would wish to learn English. If people were coming to America to worship as Lutherans instead of as Calvinists, Hilgen knew they would do so in their own tongue.

Additionally, these men must be educated and sophisticated. They would be able to understand the nuances of politics and hopefully be able to practice medicine and philosophy, and by these wielding qualities would cast a sheen of civilization over the dull finish of the frontier. The merchant princes from Charleston and their Oldenburg connections could not supply any additional candidates beyond Hilgen and Company, and so he would have to cast his gaze further afield in order to capture his prize. He would spend the years from 1845 to 1849 doing so, and doing so with the same great success that would greet most of his ventures.

This photo of the Columbia mill shows the frame construction used in the original incarnation of the Hilgen and Schroeder mill. That mill stood as a log, then frame, structure until 1855 when Hilgen and Schroeder built their stone edifice. (From the Rappold Collection.)

The first to be recruited was Frederick W. Horn. He was born on August 21, 1815, in Linum, Brandenburg, Prussia, and educated at the finest schools in the country. In fact, he was a classmate of Prince Otto von Bismark at Gray Friar's College in Berlin when studying for his law degree.

Horn wrote to friends and family that he immigrated because of a fascination with the new American nation's rapidly changing nature and its free-for-all scramble for prosperity. He came to America in 1836 at the age of 21, traveling to New York, Michigan, Illinois, Iowa, and finally settling in Mequon in 1842. He immediately became the justice of the peace, the first magistrate for Washington County, and soon the first Mequon postmaster.

The original Mequon settlers were just like their New Dubliner neighbors a couple miles away, Yankee and Irish. William T. Bonniwell, for whom today's Bonniwell Road is named, was the largest landholder and most influential of these settlers, and was decidedly Yankee in every way. While Horn liked his prospects in the area, his tumbleweed-like travels in the New World tell us that, had he not heard the siren song of German language and of a Teutonic culture being built just a few miles away, he would have eventually drifted off to another locale. Yet he did meet Hilgen, and they got on famously, and in doing so, the history of Cedarburg was irrevocably set on its course.

Horn made the move to the hamlet of Cedarburg (then still part of the larger township of Hamburg) in 1847, setting up shop as a lawyer/farmer and all-around civic leader. Accounts from the time have Horn possessing a wickedly rapacious and garrulous wit, a keen and incisive intelligence, and charisma such as few men project, and like Hilgen, was a man who stood out in any crowd. He played the perfect counterbalance to Father Hilgen as well; where Hilgen functioned as the center of Cedarburg's commercial/industrial universe, Horn stood as the political fulcrum on which the new village of Cedarburg would balance. A man of uncommon interest in public affairs, he would later in the century create and operate the community's English-speaking newspaper, one that his descendants would own and run for the next 100 years.

From James Buck's 1876 *Pioneer History of Milwaukee* we have this wonderfully descriptive, if politically biased and comma afflicted, portrait of Horn:

> This gentleman came to Milwaukee, from Posen, in the kingdom of Prussia, in 1840, and quickly became prominent in our public affairs. In person, he is tall and stout, has a large head; brown hair, dark eyes, voice loud and clear; speaks quick and distinct, with a slight German accent, and very emphatic; has a great faith in his own judgment; is a fair businessman, but likes politics better than anything else.
>
> Mr. Horn has been much in office, as a member of the State Senate and Assembly; is a good public speaker, and as presiding officer, has few equals, in this or any other state. His love for fun is unbounded, as well as for the ridiculous, and many are the practical jokes of which his associates have been the victim, that were concocted in his fertile

This photo of Frederick Horn shows his sophisticated and aristocratic bearing. He was educated alongside a German prince at the finest Prussian academy and played a major and influential role in Wisconsin politics and journalism until his death in 1893. (From the Rappold Collection.)

brain; no opening that promised any sport, ever escaped his observation. Mr. Horn has been one of the most prominent men in his county Washington, for years, and is, or was, in political faith until the last four years, an old Hunker Democrat, but of late has reformed, in that respect, and now the writer hopes to see him die in grace, which he certainly will do, if he does not backslide. Such is F. W. Horn.

For those who are curious, a Hunker Democrat was a faction within the Democratic Party during that time period. One was either "Hard" and "Soft" Democrat, or as they were more descriptively termed, the "Hunkers" and "Barnburners." This ideological split had to do with differing approaches to perceived corruption in the corporations. The Hunkers voted a straight Democratic ticket because of its firm stance against slavery despite the fact that those who ran were often perceived as soft on corruption, if not outright guilty of it. The Softs, or Barnburner Democrats, would take a more radical stance against corruption, voting with the pro-slavery Whigs or anti-slavery Republicans as it suited them (Reagan's Blue Dog Democrats spring to mind). Their name came from a popular fable about a farmer with an infestation of rodents in his barn of which he could not rid himself, so he burned the barn and all its contents to the ground.

In this heated arena, Horn took an active role in local, state, and national politics from the start. He began by convening and presiding over the formational governing body that officially made the split from Hamburg (now Grafton) in 1849. That board of supervisors consisted of himself, Hilgen, Schroeder, Groth, and a few others to lay out roads and set up school districts. Among the others who took an active part in organizing the village of Cedarburg were C.E. Chamberlain, John McGill, John Roth, John Dunne, John Smith, C. Rintelmann, Charles Dobberpuhl, J. Arndt, Rueben Wells, Michael Gorman, John Seidell, James Gafferney, Dr. H. Boclo, Dr. S. Hartwig, Edward Nolan, L.L. Sweet, and James Ruddy. By these names we can see that, while the Irish still held sway in the area, the Teutonic was on the ascendant. That would accelerate in the decade after Cedarburg was officially created.

Horn's involvement in state politics (Wisconsin became a state in 1848) went deep. He was elected to the state senate as an independent in 1848 to serve in the first legislature and was reelected senator in 1850. Thereafter, he developed a thirst for the state assembly after taking a turn as Speaker of the Assembly in 1851, which was a post he held in 1854 and 1876 as well.

In between terms as assemblyman, Horn also served the state—and Cedarburg—by acting as state commissioner of immigration. This was a post unique to Wisconsin among all the states in the union at the time. Wisconsin alone created the Commission of Immigration to aggressively promote the state to European immigrants, mainly German speakers, in an effort to fill the landscape with Teutonic settlers. The commission put out over 30,000 full color pamphlets and brochures about the state's bounty all over Europe. They heavily promoted the writing and distribution of letters home to Germany that rhapsodized over the quality of the land in Wisconsin. The commissioner and his assistants greeted immigrants as they debarked from the ships carrying them to the New World, directing them on how best to get to Wisconsin, and even sold them land while they stood on the dock. The commission also acted as a broker/banker for those families already living in America, facilitating the transfer of funds to Europe to pay for passage, and even lent money to some families (with collateral) who wanted to make the voyage to America. Horn lived and worked as Commissioner of Immigration in New York City in 1854 and 1855, steering many new immigrants to the friendly and evermore Teutonic surroundings of Cedarburg.

Another valuable recruit was B.A. Zastrow-Kussow, an intellectual and member of German nobility. He was forced to leave his homeland after the ill-fated Revolution of 1848, what came to be called a "Forty-Eighter," due to his liberal ideas and active involvement in that revolt. After spending a year in London, he found his way to Cedarburg, where he made many contributions, but none larger than his creation of the Farmers' Market Day—the first, supposedly, of its kind in the nation, and would continue for nearly 100 years. He also introduced kindergarten to Cedarburg, and later served as justice of the peace and then as state assemblyman. Zastrow-Kussow, according to one account, was "on the subject of religion . . . liberal to the extreme, discountenancing all forms of ritual. He held with others of the great German Free Thinkers, that man should not be hampered by creeds, but base his opinions on the universal law of nature."

As the Ozaukee County Historical Society's newsletter has it, Free Thinkers held a firm belief in a deity, but not in a meddling god or earthly religions, rather like the deist Founding Fathers of America, "having a belief in god-like principles in nature and a disbelief in a personal god who was interested in human feelings and welfare." Consequently, they had a great reverence for nature and the power of spirituality found therein. But due to their antagonistic attitude toward organized religion and clergy, they refused all services by clerics, usually having local magistrates and justices of the peace conduct secular baptisms, weddings, and funerals for them. One old Free Thinker farmer expired muttering these last words, "Ruf blos ein nicht pastor," or "Only don't call a pastor." Another man requested on his deathbed that, in lieu of a funeral ceremony, his friends and family take a walk in the woods. Free Thinkers were especially numerous in nearby Thiensville (where the rumor flourished that the Free Thinking founder of the colony, John Henry Thien, opposed the construction of any church, a myth that so carried the power of suggestion that no congregation had the courage to build a church there before World War I) and in the farms surrounding Cedarburg. As it turns out, the Thiensville/Cedarburg Free Thinkers were an:

Another of the Hilgen/Boerner Teutonic recruits was B.A. Zastrow-Kussow, a Free Thinker who organized the first Farmers' Market Day. Supposedly the first of its kind in the country, this tradition of gathering to trade and barter crops and information would carry on through wars and depression into the 1940s. (From the Rappold Collection.)

57

The doctor for Cedarburg from the mid-1840s through to the next century, Dr. Theodore Hartwig began his practice in Horneffers' Inn (now called the Washington House), but upon marrying, moved into the splendid cream city brick home he stands before in this photo. Hartwig played an influential role in Cedarburg's Civil War involvement. (From the Rappold Collection.)

especially active group of social and cultural organizations. Featured by their group, one to which Zastrow-Kussow would have belonged, were singing societies, an amateur dramatic club, a turnverein group, a farmer's club, and a chapter of the Grange.

There is even some speculation that Frederick Horn was a Free Thinker, given his liberal ideas, the fact that he never belonged to or attended any church, and his often stated tolerance for Free Thinking. He did, however, send his daughter to a Catholic school in Milwaukee, but those who claim Horn to be a Free Thinker rationalize that he did so in the interest of providing her the best available education, not to give her religious training.

Just after Frederick Boerner's 1846 visit to Cedarburg, a man who would become Cedarburg's doctor into the twentieth century blew through town like a maple leaf on a fall wind. Fortunately for the town, this leaf stuck to one of the many not yet cleared trees. Dr. Theodore E.F. Hartwig was freshly graduated from Marburg School of Medicine the year before and, in Milwaukee, prepared for a hunting trip when he met the same Dr. Luening who caused such trouble in the last chapter. Hartwig visited Luening in Cedarburg, lunching at Horneffer's Washington House. Horneffer, shooting the breeze with the hunting youth, asked about his circumstances and profession. Upon hearing that Hartwig was a physician, Horneffer asked that he stay in the burg as town doctor. Having but $20 in his pocket and no income, Hartwig reluctantly agreed, not really believing Cedarburg to be the best place in which to begin his practice. He settled in over the winter, and being charmed by Hilgen and Company, decided in the spring to stay.

Hartwig wrote many letters describing both his voyage to America and revealing much about what he found in the wilderness that was to become Cedarburg. He wrote home that, aside from a few scattered clearings, the area was densely wooded, so much so that he had to make his calls on foot, using a jackknife to mark a trail by which he could return (he'd apparently read the tale of Hansel and Gretel by the Grimm Brothers). Hartwig lived in and used a small room as an office and laboratory in the Washington House at a rate of $1.75 per week. Although immensely busy in that first year as the only doctor for scores of miles, one fact troubled him deeply—few people had cash to pay him.

Hartwig accepted a guaranteed salary and a large practice in the neighboring town of West Bend in 1848 only to find 17 sleighs loaded with Cedarburgers calling on him in the winter of 1849. He saw the gesture as a unanimous show of support (as indeed it must have been since 17 sleighs would have been nearly every one available to the residents of the burg). Gratified and flattered, he returned, never to leave Cedarburg again.

Hartwig, a giant of a man so hardy he never wore gloves, even in the midst of winter and on horseback, did his best to treat such dreaded frontier diseases as cholera, diphtheria, typhoid fever, small pox, pneumonia, and scarlet fever. Medical methods of the time, however, were inadequate to do the job, as gravestones from the period will testify. The best a doctor of his time could often hope to provide was some small comfort to those who were ill and to their families in the case of death.

Hartwig met and recruited Hugo Boclo to be an apothecary on a trip to Milwaukee in 1846. Boclo returned to Germany for two years (1847–1849), but also returned to the apparent charms of Cedarburg to set up an apothecary shop (on the present site of Jung's Furniture) that he manned for the next 50 years.

Meanwhile, the political situation in the area was, in a word, fluid. A territorial act of 1836 establishing Washington County made "Washington City" (now Port Washington) the county seat of justice. There were no serious objections to it, as there were no more than 20 county residents outside the township's limits at the time, and especially as there were not yet any county functions upon which to act. Yet by the time of the Act of Organization, passed by the legislature in 1840, Washington City had fallen into decline and was virtually deserted. Hamburg and Mequon, however, had "some quite thrifty neighborhoods of actual settlers," but the entire county had only 343 living white souls residing in its boundaries. Given the obvious fact that one can't place a county seat where there is no one to sit on it, the territorial government decreed that an election would take place to determine the county seat's location.

The first vote was for Hamburg, but was an empty honor for a few years, since there still wasn't much for a county government to do in the empty wilderness.

An 1846 act declared a new township system of governance, organizing all the state's counties into townships. At the same time, the act also provided for yet another vote to take place on the seat in Washington County in April 1846. In that election, Washington City got 164 votes, Hamburg 74, and Cedarburg (by this time considered by all to be a separate entity from Hamburg, but not officially so) received 100 votes. Since there was no simple majority, there was no seat awarded.

This caused a bit of turmoil and inconvenience, especially as the county was now growing rapidly and needed the services of an actual county government. According to the history of Washington and Ozaukee Counties:

> [This] whole county government was a sort of peripatetic institution, performing its functions everywhere, and having habitation nowhere. A citizen was obliged to go to one town to have his deed recorded, to another to pay his county taxes on land, to another to bring business before the County Board, and to still another for relief from the courts.

To solve the dilemma, the territorial legislature passed an act in 1847 that

These early Cedarburg residents show off not only the frame construction of their business and home but also an example of the type of horse-drawn sleigh used to collect the wayward Dr. Hartwig in 1847. (From the Robert Armbruster Archive.)

made a now more vital Washington City the county seat for five years. It wasn't a satisfactory decision for many in the county, as Washington City was quite a distance from most of the county. So while few could agree which location ought to be the seat, most agreed Washington City was definitely not the best place.

In 1848, the new state legislature washed its hands of the now tiring problem by authorizing the county to decide for itself on a site and vote yet again. Three votes were taken to narrow the choices, and in the first one, the choice was narrowed to Cedarburg, West Bend, and Washington City:

> Cedarburg being still a part of Grafton, the vote only threw the old village of Grafton out of the fight, still leaving [hope in Hamburg residents of] a chance to retain the county seat within the limits of th[at] town.
>
> On the second vote, nearly the entire vote of Grafton and the populous towns of Jackson, Mequon, and Germantown were given for Cedarburg—Washington City failed to receive as many votes as in her first trial, while nearly all the central and western towns voted for West Bend, giving her the plurality . . .

Under the law's provisions, that meant the contest would have been narrowed to Cedarburg and West Bend, but Washington City wouldn't give up the ghost, choosing instead to fight on, even if it meant resorting to dirty tactics. Civic leaders there developed a scheme to invalidate the following election, making it void. In that vote, their first line of defense was to load the ballot with false choices and 986 of the 3,700 votes cast were "for neither place" in direct contradiction of the law's provision. Ballot boxes also showed signs of having been liberally stuffed, with the preponderance of that evidence appearing in Belgium, near Washington City, where 504 "for neither place" votes were cast in a precinct which had seen only 184 and 186 votes in the prior two elections, and one of those was for president. Irregularities occurred in every town, and the whole process was considered fraudulent. While Cedarburg won, Washington City and West Bend challenged the results, embittering one and all to such an extent that ill feelings eventually led to a splintering of the county.

A letter from the Washington County Board of Supervisors written to the state legislature in late 1849 said, in part, that the citizens of the county simply could not determine the location of the seat, and asked the legislature to "establish a permanent location for the county seat, and thus relieve the county from the embarrassment and inconvenience of its present situation."

The legislature responded with a surprise when it divided the county into north and south. The south would be called Tuskola and contained Mequon, Grafton, Germantown, Erin, Jackson, Polk, and Hartford, with Cedarburg possessing the seat. All else would stay in Washington County and Washington City would hold the seat. The citizens of the new county of Tuskola were then asked for an up or down vote on its existence in 1850. This move proved even more unpopular than the previously unsettled situation, so most cities voted only under protest and overwhelmingly against, 1,991–276, or nearly 10–1 (a margin that held true in every precinct except Cedarburg, which voted against only at 102–174).

In the meantime, the state's chief justice decreed that a permanent courthouse be built in Washington City because it was still the county seat of record, buttressing the city's claims to be the de facto, if not de jure, Washington County seat. Later, in 1852 when Washington City's five-year term expired, the seat moved to Grafton with an addendum added that a vote would be taken after the first meeting of the Board of Supervisors on whether to remove the seat to West Bend, but no other place. So Cedarburg and Washington City, the two main instigators in the previous battles, were knocked out of contention (or so they thought) by a disgusted legislature.

That vote, on the question of moving the seat to West Bend, failed by over 700 of the 4,300 votes cast. The entire sorry situation upset every community, so the legislative session in both houses of 1853 was inundated with lobbyists, letters, petitions, affidavits, remonstrances, applications for relief, and anything else local civil leaders could conceive. The struggle had gone on for 13 years and by now was seen as an evil that needed excising by a higher power since the communities themselves could never agree. Powerful West Bend and Washington City lobbies put forward an east/west division scheme that was reluctantly, but then gladly, implemented by both houses (once lawmakers saw surcease of the dilemma) to make the two towns the county seats. Ironically, Washington City was split off from its namesake county, Washington, and took over as the seat of a new Ozaukee (Indian for "yellow-earth") County, the smallest of Wisconsin's counties.

None of this could have pleased Hilgen and Company greatly, but they were encouraged that Cedarburg was rapidly becoming the spoke around which the new county's wheel spun agriculturally, commercially, and industrially. Demographically speaking, the area changed considerably as many of the original Irish settlers in and around Cedarburg sold out to Northern Germans following Captain Rohr and Johannes Grabau. The community began to take on a decidedly German cast, and while not yet nearly exclusively German-speaking, was well on the way to becoming so, as indicated by the uproar into which Cedarburg would wade over German-language instruction and the teaching of religion (Lutheranism, of course) in public schools.

Presaging twentieth-century controversies over religious instruction, Wisconsinites of the time bitterly debated the role of language and religion in the schoolroom. These new German-speaking immigrants were scrupulously faithful to their Lutheran ideals and taught them in both their religious and public schools, seeing nothing wrong with it. For instance, all state public schools in Prussia, which all children ages five to twelve went to by law, emphasized religion first and foremost. Two main Teutonic/Lutheran purposes lay underneath this instruction, whether it was public or private instruction—the teaching of the catechism to youth and nurturing the language and German culture. An 1876 article in *Schultzeitung*, Wisconsin Synod's official publication, drove the latter point home, "Our parochial schools should also be the nurseries of the German

Although Cedarburg was the commercial and farming hub of the county, as this picture of Market Day shows, it could not overcome political machinations and skullduggery by other communities to become the political and judicial seat of the county. (From the Rappold Collection.)

Language. The German school and church have the duty to help perpetuate our beloved mother tongue."

The new state of Wisconsin banned sectarian education in public schools, but unfortunately neglected to define "sectarian," which allowed state superintendents of instruction wide latitude in the matter. These superintendents contended the question of teaching religion in a public school was moot as long as instruction followed a vague non-sectarian line. This was described as the teaching of "broader and sublimer sentiments such as the relationship between God and man, man to God, and world-wide truths" held by all faiths. The superintendents therefore tried to please everyone, guaranteeing that few would be pleased.

That being the predominant official attitude, articles in the *Wisconsin Journal of Education* (the official organ of the State Department of Public Instruction) and policies at the state level advocated a laissez faire approach to religious teaching in public school. This was the status quo until 1860, when Cedarburg Free Thinkers spoke their mind with a unified voice by writing an article for the journal. The letter astounded many, especially in very Lutheran Cedarburg, as the writers called for abolishing all religious instruction in public schools, including bible reading and prayer.

The article, entitled "Moral and Religious Instruction," written by Cedarburg's own forty-eighter and Free Thinker, B.A. Zastrow-Kussow, raised the following question: "If now, in a commonwealth like ours, men of different religions have the same rights, as citizens, how is it possible for any religious instruction to be

This scene depicts early Cedarburg's Fire House, which stood where today a lawn leads to City Hall (itself a former school). The lot once housed a frame building containing the public "Free School." (From the Rappold Collection.)

given in the common schools?" The author raises an almost contemporary point by contending that every religion was sectarian when compared with another (or none). In her doctoral thesis entitled *The Americanization of German Immigrants: Language, Religion, and Schools in Nineteenth Century Wisconsin*, Susan Jean Kuyper states:

> Because these theologically conservative Lutherans were not convinced of the existence of the body of common, undisputed, and universally embraced religious truths which public school supporters cited as the basis for daily bible reading and prayer in the schools, they were able to see that Christianity itself might seem sectarian to some persons. Even if there were certain tenets which were common to all Christian sect[s], these tenets would still be considered sectarian to non-Christians, and on those grounds they should be banned from the public schools altogether. Viewed from this perspective of a non-Christian, Christianity itself was a sect, even if the religious principles being espoused were not distinctively those of Methodism, Presbyterianism, or Congregationalism. If, as Superintendent of Schools Lyman C. Draper had asserted, "Christianity was everywhere incorporated in the law of the land," then, according to the group in Cedarburg, it was unfortunately true that sectarianism, too was everywhere incorporated in the law of the land. To all those who agreed with this group of Cedarburg residents, the constitutional ban on sectarian education in the

public schools required nothing short of a guarantee that religion would have no place whatsoever, in any form, in public education.

Some issues die hard; the Supreme Court listened to precisely the same argument when it heard a case about prayer at high school football games in 2000.

The battle over religious instruction (and therefore, to Lutherans, a battle over language) raged in Cedarburg and in Wisconsin, causing many German- and English-speaking parents alike to remove their children from schools. Frederick Horn, in his 1863 report as superintendent of schools, said he found that people demanded German instruction and they pressured him to hire German-speaking instructors. However, he found the English language qualifications of many would-be German-speaking instructors suspect.

In Cedarburg's first school, a venture begun by Trinity Church and shared by many in the village, it was all-Deutsch-all-the-time, just as it was in the village at large. The public, or "Free," school that began in 1854 had what we modern-day Americans would call bilingual education, with some classes taught in English, while the majority were taught in German. The parochial schools in Cedarburg would all be known well into the twentieth century as "the German Schools."

Meanwhile, the city grew in leaps and bounds. In 1848, the new state legislature chartered the Milwaukee to Fon Du Lac Plank Road, which to the joy of Hilgen and Company went right through downtown Cedarburg. It had three toll stations along its route, one being just south of Cedarburg. Later that year, another plank and macadam (crushed gravel) road was built west from nearby Ulao (which had a port at the time) and went through Grafton, Cedarburg, and on to Hartford.

The first frame house took shape also in 1847. Most people had used logs, yet a few families like Groth's used the easily accessible fieldstone or quarried stone. Dr. Hartwig describes how Cedarburg's first frame building went up in this excerpt from a letter:

In the same year (1847) I began building my house, a so-called frame house as they are customarily built here where there is no building stone. The entire house is constructed of boards. Beams, three or four inches thick, cut at the saw mill, form the skeleton. Over these, boards 3/4 inch thick are nailed like room tiles, one overlapping the other The roof is covered with one inch thick boards and over these are nailed shingles of leather or cedar wood. Flooring, windows, and doors are here made by machine and expensive.

Stores opened as well during this time. William Vogenitz from Magdeburg, Prussia arrived in Cedarburg after stints in Milwaukee, Watertown, and Mequon to open a general merchandise store. He also served in the state assembly in 1856 and became justice of the peace, serving for many years. Another general store started to supply the area with manufactured goods when Juergen Schroeder came from Charleston to Cedarburg in 1851 to improve his health, as he too suffered from the swampy climate and was in fear of contracting yellow fever. He became postmaster in 1856 (appointed by President Buchanan) and his business served as the town center in those days—as post office, gathering place, and news collecting, aside from the typical business transactions. Very little money exchanged hands as most of the trade was barter.

Hilgen purchased 74 acres of land to the east of town in 1852, developing it into a day spa called Hilgen Spring Resort and Park. He capitalized on the natural springs on the wild land that bordered the creek and was almost half untouched forest to create a resort Milwaukeeans and Chicagoans descended upon to reinvigorate themselves. Hilgen:

> . . . laid out a park with walks, drives, fountains, bridges, and flower gardens. Encouraged by the visitors who flocked there to drink the pure mineral water [a very Teutonic thing to do, even in today's Germany], he built two hotels with dining rooms, a tavern, a band stand and a bath house, which was placed under the supervision of Dr. H. A. Jaergens. [The] Gala opening . . . featured a Cedarburg Band Concert in the afternoon and a ball in the evening.

Hilgen and Schroeder also rebuilt the mill's dam, which had been damaged by high water, in 1855. In the same year, they began construction on a new five-story,

This view of Hilgen's mill is from the south. Five stories tall with walls nearly 3 feet thick, the building would have made a fine defensive bastion in a war-torn Europe. As it is, it represents one of the finest examples of Greek Revival architecture in a Midwest mill. (Courtesy of the Robert Armbruster Archive.)

Here is the mill as it looks today from the east. This photo shows the side of the mill that contained the millrace and amply demonstrates that the mill, 150 years after construction, is still one of the most beautiful buildings in Wisconsin.

Greek Revival–style, stone and mortar mill on the same site as their previous log and frame structure stood. It was said to have cost $22,000, the equivalent of $400,000 in today's market, which is no small sum. They used stone as it was a readily available material and a bit cooler to work in than log or frame structures. Plus it reduced the threat of catastrophic fire (all lighting and heating at the time was flame of some sort, whale oil, later kerosene, or homemade tallow candles).

Much of the stone came from the creek below, which was diverted to expose its bottom, and was "cut and hauled up a tramway 'by muscle power,' one man pulling and another pushing." To build the upper floors an earthen works was formed that spanned from roughly the spot where Horneffer's Hotel and Schroeder's store sit a block away, then stone blocks were pulled up by mules or oxen to be put into place by masons. As the building grew toward the sky, so too did the earthen berm, until it stood four and a half stories high, matching the height of the building.

Acknowledged as one of the most beautiful mills ever built in Wisconsin, the steep roof adorning it is called a clerestory, or monitor roof—a style that had been in use for some years because it increased the amount of light flowing into the space below. Another impressive detail includes the brick walls just under the roof; the difference in color to the limestone is so microscopic that one can hardly tell it is made of a different material. After the mill was finished, a three-story building was erected across the street containing a feed and flour store.

Several other stone or brick structures were created between 1849 and 1860. Three fine examples are John Schuette Sr.'s odd little cracker box-style residence in 1855, the Central House Hotel in 1853, and Henry C. Nero's hostelry, which boasted "First class accommodations, choice wines, liquors, and cigars. Good stabling and large stock yard." George Fischer built the Kuhefuss House in 1849, but sold it to Ed Blank later in the year when he left to join the California gold rush. The German Free School was constructed in 1855 as a dance hall before Trinity made it a school.

John Weber Sr., a stone mason, arrived in Cedarburg in 1859 and worked on many a building through 1862 until he partnered with Dr. Fricke and began operating the Cedarburg Brewery on the west side of the creek. He ran it alone after Fricke's death in 1865, making almost all of the beer that locals consumed. He sold it by the barrel to hotels, saloons, and stores, who in turn would peddle it on site or by the bucket to households (giving rise to the phrase recalled by children who "ran the bucket"). At its height, the brewery employed six men and produced 2,300 barrels of beer each year until Prohibition forced them into soda water; it eventually closed.

With the addition of a hotel, a brewer, and the beer gardens of Hilgen Spring Park, along with its own school district and post office, Cedarburg was now a complete political entity and a vital growing community—and a Teutonic one at that. Messrs. Hilgen, Boerner, and Schroeder not only brought together all the elements needed to duplicate the German burg on American soil, they oversaw the process of carving a Lutheran village from the forest. The village would continue to grow, but only "just so," and in the Teutonic way.

YOU WANT FRESH AIR

And plenty of it, charming surroundings and rural quiet where the tired nerves can rest and the mind be entirely free from business cares. You are looking for Health, Pleasure and Comfort --- for a place where you may recuperate enjoying the beauties of nature, all these you find abundantly at . . . .

Hilgen's Spring Summer Resort.

Frederick Hilgen knew that work must be leavened by recreation, and to Teutons of the day, that meant spring water, outdoors, and good food and drink. The Hilgen Spring Resort fulfilled those needs, and the needs of those in far-off urban locations such as Chicago and Milwaukee. The resort would become one of the leading destinations in the Midwest in the mid- to late-nineteenth century. (From the Wirth Family Archive.)

6. Panic, War, Riot, and the Iron Horse

As far as the eye could see north and south there was a string of galloping horses drawing wagons so close that the heads of one team almost touched the rear of the wagon ahead.
    –Eyewitness account of the Great Indian Scare in the
    History of the Town of Mequon

Civic leaders in Cedarburg welcomed word of a plank road's construction through their town, but they were well aware that this alone wouldn't be sufficient to fulfill their needs. What the village needed was rail service, and soon. Father Hilgen set about negotiating for its arrival and succeeded eventually. But first the village would fall prey to an industry's greed, the economic Panic of 1857, the Indian Scare of 1862, and the disruption of war.

Being that the dozens of railways cropping up across the state found bank financing scarce in those days, farmers along the line purchased stock in the railroads to pay for laying down the tracks. When the Milwaukee & Superior Railroad began constructing a line along the lakefront in 1856, Hilgen and Company saw opportunity dancing before their eyes. Nearly every Cedarburg farmer who could afford to do so bought "subscriptions" to the new rail line, often mortgaging their property to raise the cash. Boerner, Hilgen, Schroeder, Groth, and Malone are just a few names included in a long list, one far beyond what space allows in this book. The line grew slowly toward Mequon until 1857 when Panic froze all operations. Immediately it was discovered that the president of the Milwaukee & Superior had absconded with $80,000 capitalization, much of it the farmers' money.

It appears that even before the Panic and theft, in the unscrupulous way some railroad speculators went about their business, the Milwaukee & Superior hadn't planned to actually finish the line. The track stopped just short of Mequon and the grumbling farmers holding subscriptions campaigned for completion, so the railroad actually put them to work and had them grade the bed going through town.

The farmers showed up with horses, graders, teams, even hired Indian hands, and worked at it for a week. That Saturday evening when they sought payment from the promoters they discovered the railroad men had left town, never to be seen again.

The Milwaukee & Superior went bankrupt soon after the theft, leaving many thousands of dollars in mortgages for the victimized farmers and merchants to pay off. It would be 14 more years before Cedarburg was connected to the big city port by iron horse. William F. Raney wrote the following in a 1936 article in the *Wisconsin Magazine of History:*

> Besides the municipalities, the railroads exploited private citizens, especially the farmers who so much desired their facilities. Between 1850 and 1857 some 6000 Wisconsin farmers mortgaged their farms for a total of $5,000,000. The agents of the companies gave stock certificates to the farmers in exchange for the mortgages which they immediately sold to investors in the eastern states. Then in the panic of 1857 every railroad in the state went into bankruptcy, and the farmers were left with a lot of worthless paper. Compromise and legislation did something to remedy this situation in the decade before the civil war, but it has remained one of the most painful episodes in the history of railroad finance.

Looming larger than the fear of losing money to unscrupulous speculators, in the minds of many new immigrants, was the fear of the Native American. This apprehension came to a climax in August 1862 after the Great Sioux Uprising in Minnesota. The Sioux vented their anger and frustration with federal Indian policy by burning entire families in their cabins, nailing children to doors, raping children (one story has a dozen men doing so before hacking a girl to pieces), and dismembering babies before throwing their remains into the faces of their mothers.

They spread across an area including the Redwood (Indian) Agency and a German town called New Ulm in Minnesota, devastating the countryside and causing wholesale panic. They were, however, soon brought under control by federal troops, yet the rumors of uprising still spread like wildfire across the state. Panic ensued from Manitowac (in the center of the state) all the way to Milwaukee. The month of August saw report after report of uprisings, and each one proved false. In fact, there were only about 9,000 Native Americans still in the state at the time, many of them loyal and dedicated Americans who were even away fighting for the Union Army at the time. They themselves responded to reports with panic of their own, knowing from experience that a frightened white man was a dangerous white man.

One history called the rash of false reports a Confederate plot to destroy the amity between native and settler populations, and if it worked, the scheme would have been replayed in other states. Few today give the assertion credence and the incidents most likely happened naturally, but it serves to underscore the intense anxiety people felt in those days of settlement and war. The notion that Native Americans were every bit as frightened as whites is evidenced by Captain Harrison, whom Governor Salomon sent to investigate the rumors of uprisings. He wrote, "So far as I can judge, the fear is mutual, and the Indians and Whites are striving to outdo each other in conceding territory—that is, while the Whites are running one way, the Indians are running the other." His perceptive appraisal of the situation, however, didn't reach the ears of isolated farmers, and the panic continued.

Rumors on September 4 began to trickle into Milwaukee and the bluish haze on the horizon was mistaken for smoke. By evening, wagon loads of settlers began arriving in Milwaukee filled with people screaming, "The Injuns are coming!" The town chairman of Richfield, north of Milwaukee, sent a telegram to troops in Milwaukee stating, "Please send us troops with arms by the first train. The Indians are within five miles of here and are murdering and burning everything they come across. They burned Cedarburg last night."

In Cedarburg, confusion reigned as farmers rode into town reporting massacres on neighboring plots, the burning of the Catholic church (then southwest of town), and other equally horrible disasters. Wagons met coming from opposite

The rush to create a network of steel tying the grain producing areas of the great American West to the major urban centers also brought a rush of speculation and corruption. The Milwaukee & Superior Railroad was one line that was built on speculation and brought down by corruption. Here a team lays track, a track that made it as far north as Mequon, stopping short of Cedarburg by some miles. (From the Rappold Collection.)

directions, both claiming that the Indians were right behind them. Some said they had drank too much firewater, causing some bar owners to put out kegs in hopes of quieting the raging natives. Farm wagons came racing into town, the horses stinking of sweat, farmer and family pale and shaking with fright. Some wagons just went right through town, the drivers screaming in German, "The Indians are coming, flee for your lives!" Many people loaded their children into wagons and headed for Milwaukee or Port Washington, with some holed up in the five-story stone mill, hoping that the nearly 3-foot-thick walls would protect them.

Charles Chamberlain, a farmer in Cedarburg working his land near where a thresher was being operated that day, wrote this account:

> The hum of the machine, the crack of the whip, the commanding tones of the men, all seemed to point to the fact that they were masters of the situation. All of a sudden there was a great commotion among the men. The machine ceased its whir, and in less time than it takes to tell it, the horses were released from the power, hitched to the wagon, turned into the road, when they came tearing toward my house, the men yelling amid the great excitement, "Indians! Escape for your lives! The Indians are coming." Down the road they went, pell mell, and as far as I could distinguish them in the cloud of dust, they were swinging their hats and coats yelling, "Indians! Fly for your lives, Indians!"

Assorted stories tell us the rush was so great people lost or forgot children. One Cedarburg farmer arrived in Port Washington to find one of his kids had fallen unnoticed out of a wagon. Another man found on arrival in Milwaukee that he had loaded someone else's children into his wagon. Concerning cash, Ulrich Landoldt gave an account of his neighbor deciding to bury a box of money in the garden to keep it from the Indians. When he returned the next day he discovered the box—still full—sitting on the ground next to the hole he'd dug and filled. One man drove his sweating team into Brown Deer to find he had lost the rear of his wagon, which happened to contain his wife and furniture. Another man reported witnessing "maimed horses and broken wagons" on the road to Brown Deer.

One realizes from this eyewitness account by Reverend Robert Graez, pastor at Trinity Church in Cedarburg, that the panic slowly came to a boil overnight:

> We had just finished our evening meal on Sept. 3 when a man came riding into town on horseback, shouting that thousands of Indians were starting an uprising and had sworn to kill all the white settlers in Wisconsin. The Indians were reported to be in Sheboygan, thirty miles away, burning houses and murdering inhabitants. It was believed that they could be in Cedarburg by three in the morning. The rider was on his way to Milwaukee to summon the aid of the soldiers stationed there.
>
> After he had left, the men of the town assembled for a conference.

The fear of Indian attack was both real and inflamed. Woodcuts such as this one were published in the aftermath of real attacks on white settlers by Native Americans tired of being pushed to relocate. However, this kind of dramatic rendition also struck unreasoning fear into the hearts of many settlers, especially the burghers newly nestled on the banks of Cedar Creek.

They decided not to flee, but to collect all the firearms and take up strategic positions in Cedarburg. Many of the women and children were sent to the Mill for greater protection. Between one and two in the morning wagons filled with women and children began to pass through Cedarburg. Men were on foot or on horseback. Some of these people had come twenty-two miles, and they reported that the Indians had been only two miles from their homes and were burning everything in their pathway. At three in the morning teacher Kuehn and his family came to the parsonage. I comforted the women and children with the words of the 124th Psalm. By noon, everyone was more calm. They believed the report might be false, or if true, that the soldiers would reach Cedarburg before the Indians came.

Just then a cry went up in the streets that the Indians were only two miles away, and had set fire to the Catholic Church. Farm people, who were now fleeing into Cedarburg had seen great clouds of smoke. Many from Cedarburg now started for Milwaukee, and we decided that if our neighbors left, we would go with them. We learned that several babies had been born prematurely on the flight to Milwaukee. Two thousand wagons filled the streets of that city, and the friendly Indians living there had fled. The entire day of Sept. 4 (my wife's birthday) was filled with terror. To add to the misery of the refugees, rain fell in torrents.

A man "in all sincerity" reported to the *Milwaukee Sentinel* that he saw Indians stream from the woods as he and his family escaped; he claimed they set fire to his home. The Ozaukee County Historical Society's newsletter states that:

> People loaded stoves, pots, kettles, food supplies, and furniture into wagons and plunged headlong into disorganized flight. In many cases they destroyed all the property they were unable to take, not wanting to leave anything of value to the Indians. Flour was dumped into rivers, whiskey poured on the ground, pigs and other livestock were driven into houses and barns to feast on the precious stores.

Governor Salomon ordered the state militia, headed by Captain Charles Lehman, to march to Cedarburg and confront the Indians. Two army companies moved north to intercept the bands of natives, meeting only three along the way: a squaw with a baby in a papoose and a sickly man sleeping near the creek. When they arrived in Cedarburg on September 5, they found only barrels of beer in the streets and doors opened to the air (making for a proper foraging, since marching is hungry work). So instead of discovering Indians, the soldiers soon found themselves with indigestion from eating all the German treats. Another contingent of troops who came from Waukesha pawned their rifles that evening and stayed to drink the night away as only Germans could.

Reverend Graez expressed great relief upon seeing the soldiers:

Every person responded with dread and determination when they saw this woodcut, published in a German-speaking newspaper in 1862 after the New Ulm Uprising in Minnesota.

No one had seen any unfriendly Indians, yet the inhabitants of five or six counties were fleeing before them. On the morning of September 5, two companies of soldiers came from Milwaukee. They were given the best accommodations Cedarburg had to offer. Two were quartered with us—a 57-year old man with a long white beard, who was a doctor of philosophy named Franz Joseph Felsecker from Bamburg, Germany, and a young man, Peter Divoschek, from Neuhaus, Austria. In the afternoon I called on a sick man who had been left helpless and alone when everyone in his family had left for Milwaukee. People are now beginning to return to their homes.

The soldiers went home the next day, ridiculing the returning and sheepish residents for their foolish panic and unreasoning fears. The citizens became so irate they nearly mobbed the soldiers as they marched out of town. One person admitted later that the settlers were "ridiculous, frightened, desperate, foolish, cowardly . . . ." The Ozaukee County Historical Society's historian wrote:

Gradually people began to realize that the only thing they had been fleeing from was their own fear. They began to feel a little foolish, then very foolish, about the whole thing. Many hated to admit to their true reason for coming to Milwaukee. A typical scene between two "auslanders" would run something like this: "Wie gehts, August! What are you doing here? You didn't believe those silly stories about the Indians, did you?" "Naturlich, nein. Ich? Afraid of Indians? Nien Herman, I chust came in to do a little shopping." "So? But August, why did you bring the cow?" "Oh that? Vell, I brought it for—for the same reason you brought your parlor melodeon."

The *Milwaukee Sentinel* thought the whole affair hilarious. They ran a long series of satires on the "Battle of Fort Cedarburg," which so infuriated Captain Lehman that he burst into the offices of the paper and drubbed the writer of the series with his scabbard. Captain Lehman may have gained some "closure" in beating the writer, but Cedarburg residents failed to put the episode completely behind them, as will be seen later.

The Cedarburg area grew prosperous in the years before the Civil War, with many new arrivals from Germany clearing land and making farms. Being fresh from Germany, a place where internecine warfare took place with great regularity, these immigrants couldn't quite comprehend that Americans would do battle with one another. If another foreign power were invading, that would have been another matter. Besides, many of the immigrants had come to America to avoid conscription into the King's army in the first place. They weren't about to leave their barely cleared land to fight a war that had little or nothing to do with them. So when Fort Sumter was fired upon, the call to arms was but a whimper in Cedarburg.

As this photo from the period suggests, Cedarburg farmers and businessmen were far more interested in making a prosperous and secure life where they were than in making war on people elsewhere. This traffic jam occurred with regularity—every fourth Monday—even through the Civil War. (From the Rappold Collection.)

"The enthusiasm of the German settlers in the United States for the Civil War and for the Abolition movement has too often been exaggerated, and the doings and sayings of the few taken to represent the views of the many," wrote John Hawgood in *The Tragedy of German-America*. Indeed, to these newly-arrived German-speakers, Prohibition and sabbatarianism (legislating Yankee-style practices on the Sabbath) eroded the spirit of liberty as much as slavery, and were issues that affected Germans far more directly. Even though Frederick Hilgen, as a state senator in 1860, railed against the institution of slavery in the statehouse, stating, "There is no right of interference with slavery in the slave states by legislation in the Free States; however, the government was formed for the declared purpose of 'Preserving the blessings of Liberty,' " war over slavery was a tough sell in Cedarburg. Residents didn't care about the long-running battle over the extension of slavery to new territories. Their main concern was building a community based on their Teutonic culture. Besides, Cedarburg and the surrounding areas were a Democratic bastion. In the 1864 presidential election, George McClellan received 2,056 in Ozaukee County to 242 for Republican President Abraham Lincoln.

When Governor Randall called for rifle companies from around the state to volunteer in the first weeks, there was much opposition and apathy, especially in those regions with German immigrants who had voted overwhelmingly against the Republicans. When the Cedarburg Rifle Company was asked, it publicly refused to enlist. According to the Ozaukee County Historical society newsletter:

> [Frederick] Horn, a prominent Democrat, had incurred the animosity of the Republican press when he was a member of the legislature, and when he refused to join [the war], they attacked him. Editors assailed him as disloyal, and Horn answered the charges in a letter to the governor in which he charged that the Republicans were to blame for the war which he hoped could be averted, and he said his family did not want him to join, and anyway, he was too old. However, he said this was a secondary consideration.

By the third week of the war, attitudes were changing, although only slightly; the community began to begrudgingly accept the war as a fact and that they belonged on the Union's side by virtue of geography, if not politics. Horn made no more public effort to impede involvement in the war, but privately must have been very influential, given the limited number of Cedarburg residents who eventually enlisted and served.

John Hawgood writes that many German "volunteers were single men who could not find suitable work elsewhere, and they often sought the least difficult track. As a rule the German volunteer was following the path of least resistance." In the now burgeoning community of Cedarburg, the path of least resistance would have been towards the fields, not to war. It sent only 23 enlisted men to serve, which is telling, since Fredonia (less than half the size) sent 52, Belgium 38, Grafton 71 (of equal size), Mequon 65, Port Washington 95, and Saukville 43. All the towns in the county, even the smallest, sent far more soldiers than did Cedarburg.

Many factors fed the resistance to armed service by Cedarburg Teutons. Since the German speakers resisted learning English, the only source of information they had were German newspapers. Many of these publications actually championed slavery while shielded from wrath of authorities behind the German language in which they wrote. For the most part, the German press blamed the North, and above all the abolitionists, for not compromising on an issue of little importance to their readership. The papers openly spoke of the states' right to rebel, about the classism inherent in enlistment and conscription, and the power of wealth to avoid conscription by paying for a substitute. These last sentiments especially rubbed German speakers the wrong way, as it appeared they were being taken advantage of by rulers who wanted to use them as cannon fodder. Others reminded citizens who were still nervous that while this last scare proved to be a false alarm, the Native Americans might still attack vulnerable families while the men were off in battle.

Still, large numbers of German radicals, Forty-Eighters, Protestant liberals, Turners, and Free Thinkers generally rallied to support the antislavery cause and adopted pro-Union, Republican, and Lincoln stances, largely because of their previous struggles for social reform in Europe. In fact, many of the volunteers in the two purely German regiments formed in Wisconsin were members of the Lederkranz and its rival musical society, the Liedertafel.

Yet classism, manifesting itself in conscription, drove Cedarburg residents and their neighbors to erupt violently in the Draft Riot of 1862. The wealthy and connected could afford to purchase substitutions for themselves and family members, and did so. Unscrupulous "agents" had recently come through the

Despite the misgivings felt by most Cedarburg residents, some men did fight in the Union Army. This 1863 photo of Wirth relative William Roebken Sr. shows a proud fighting man ready to do his new country proud. (From the Wirth Family Collection.)

county selling farmers "immunity" from service, only to pocket the cash and leave its victims prey to the draft. The members of the Draft Board responsible for conscription in Ozaukee County were Masons, and the Alt Lutheraner German and Catholic Luxembourger farmers in the area viewed such secret secular societies with deep suspicion. They also perceived that the board members saw themselves as an "aristocracy," making a call to arms and expecting quick and obsequious compliance by the "peasantry." To make matters worse, the official examining surgeon, Dr. Hartwig, who months earlier began his work of developing preliminary medical fitness examinations, appeared to some to be exempting otherwise healthy men who had power, influence, or wealth. There may well have been some truth to their assertions; an investigation of the Civil War rolls resulted in the discovery very few leading family's names.

The first conscription was scheduled for November 10, 1862. On that day, the draft commissioner, William Pors (a close friend of Hartwig's), arrived at the county courthouse in (now) Port Washington to begin drafting names for service. Upon arrival, he and his assistants were seized by a mob said to number nearly 1,000. The mob destroyed the draft rolls, dragged Pors through the front door of the courthouse, and threw him down the steps to the street, causing considerable injury. The crowd then pelted him with rocks while he ran to the post office and concealed himself in a cellar. The rioters followed, but could not gain access, so they went to his nearby home and demolished the interior. They then divided into two separate mobs, one of which went to a local store owner and compelled him to paint "No Draft" on his windows. They destroyed the interiors of at least a half-dozen homes, mostly of prominent Port Washington citizens and Masons.

Some cooler heads in the mob convinced a local printer, John Bohan, editor of the *Ozaukee County Advertiser*, to print a large banner saying "No Draft; No Destruction of Property," to little effect. Part of the mob seized a 4-pound cannon and loaded it with the one and only ball they could find. They wheeled it out onto the town's single pier and defied Uncle Sam to come arrest them.

Word of the disturbance got to Madison and Milwaukee by telegraph, and Governor Salomon sent in the 28th Regiment from Milwaukee, half of whom used steamboat to go as far as Ulao, marching up on the rioters' flank, and the other half directly into Port's harbor, blocking the mob's escape. They quelled the riot peaceably, making 120 arrests. These men were taken to Camp Randall and released a few months later. While no record exists of their names, nor of those involved in the riot, one can confidently assume that Cedarburg residents were present and involved.

Records do, however, exist depicting who from Cedarburg was drafted and who served—and also who deserted. The government was having trouble finding a sufficient number of troops, so they paid large bounties to volunteers enlisting in the Union Army. In July 1862, the going rate was one quarter of a $100 bounty in advance at the time of mustering in, with the remainder payable when mustering out. Many recruits were offered an additional premium of $2 or $3, and this was all in addition to the pay of approximately $13 per month (during this time the average week's pay was under $10).

In the pockets of most soldiers the $27 or $28, plus their first weeks' pay (most compensation was issued quarterly or monthly), would weigh heavily on their minds as they wondered, why risk life and limb when they could go home and invest the cash in their farms? In Pennsylvania alone, over 24,000 men deserted. Some bounty deserters would accept $300 to substitute for a merchant or landowner and appear for induction, only to desert a few days later. They would then go through the same process in another location, making a killing, so to speak.

The draft over which Ozaukee County residents rioted netted only 50 Union Army conscripts countywide, and most of those deserted. For example, every single Cedarburger drafted into the 34th Infantry that November escaped service within weeks of reporting for duty. Carl Jonas, Lawrence Janssen, Henry Schmidt, Friederich Spille, William Deinert, John Helmke, George Howard, Carl Moldenhauer, Richard Carroll, Frederick Behrens, and Frederick Bliesner all deserted solely or in pairs between December 10, 1862 and January 28, 1863.

The only non-deserting Cedarburg resident in the company, Gottlieb Buch, found a substitute for himself on January 14, and the 34th Regiment, Ozaukee County's own, went to war without a Cedarburger. Another group of dissenters, known as War Democrats, served under duress. One of these War Democrats joined the Union Army, but later expressed his cynicism about its goals and aims in a letter to his wife in Grafton: "Dearest, take my word for it, the whole war from beginning to end is nothing but humbug and a swindle."

Yet there were men from the area who served the Union Army and the Republican President Lincoln by struggling to help unify the country. Take, for example, the 26th Regiment, Company A, a German-speaking group from Ozaukee County. Charles Gottschalk served as a wagoner, a trade he learned in the 26th and later put to good use. He continued teaming after his discharge, hauling flour to Milwaukee for two and a half years. He then began his livery business in Cedarburg and soon had the largest one in Ozaukee County, housing a stable of 20 horses and many fine carriages and sleighs.

William Maetzgold served in the same company as Gottschalk and was captured by Confederate troops; he served out the war at Chancellorsville prison camp. Other Cedarburg residents served in the 26th Regiment, Company A, including: Milliam Mueller, who served for more than two and a half years before being wounded and later discharged in February 1865; Michael Moldenhauer, who was wounded at Averysboro; Henry Roth, who served as a sergeant with distinction without accruing any injury; and William and Henry Rintelmann, who both fought at and were imprisoned after Gettysburg, and when mustered out in 1865 were ill and still recovering. Space doesn't allow a complete rundown on each man's service, but suffice it to say most of the men who served did so with distinction and valor.

Besides the singular effects on these men's individual lives, the war also created change in the commercial growth of Cedarburg and the lives of the townsfolk. One change, the sudden lack of planed wood for frame houses, forced an adjustment in the style of construction, replacing with stone the frame that residents had begun using. Since the war consumed every board that could be milled and stone was abundant in the area, residents switched to building with rock. Most of the homes constructed during this time and after the war were "rubble" construction, a technique not unlike today's use of poured concrete in which a wall-shaped mold, or box, is created and mortar is poured into it along with smallish stones, called rubble, creating a durable material. The faces of buildings created for downtown businesses were often finished with cornices and hand-carved stone, but a glance at their sides reveals that rubble construction was the rule.

Most of the early businessmen responsible for building these stores lived with their families in apartments above with no closeting, thus great armoires were used for storage. The lots along "Main Street," as Washington Avenue was called then, were long and narrow so they could accommodate the necessary coal shed, bin, barn, or garden. One account describes a vibrant and vital Cedarburg during this time:

> [Homes were] built close to the street, leisure hours were spent sitting on front porches protected from traffic by white picket fences. If a home was located near a saloon, the fence might need frequent repair, however. This was often the case on the last Monday of each month, Cattle Fair Day—or Fair Day. The German farmers and the Irish would meet as friends and barter with one another, but as the day wore on they would get drunk, often ending up fighting and pouring into the street to strip the fences of pickets to use as weapons.

This early Cedarburg photo shows the use of wood in main and outbuildings. The Civil War required all the wood that could be milled, leaving residents of Cedarburg little choice but to begin using the readily available Niagara Limestone and the inexpensive and distinctive cream city brick that dominates today's downtown. (From the Rappold Collection.)

The town in this period was really just a huge farm garnished with shops and gristmills along a main street. Every house had farm animals in its barn and pastures extending westward up to the hill where the high school now stands. That area, between what is now St. John Street and Madison Avenue, was known as Velvet Street for its smoothly nibbled grass. Each home had at least two cows for milk and butter, plenty of chickens for eggs, and a few horses used for transportation. Summer kitchens were built outdoors, but as close to the indoor version as possible, and had large built-in brick ovens with cauldrons by their sides. The cooking would begin before dawn and continue throughout the day, with breads being placed in the ovens at night to bake.

The Civil War increased the need for production of a wide range of goods, from the buttons to grains from the mills, a fact not lost on Hilgen and Company. Dietrich Wittenberg, Hilgen's son-in-law and employee, used Hilgen money and that of Joseph Trottman to build a mill to manufacture wool goods for the military. Finished in 1865, it missed much of the war trade, but prospered nonetheless. It too was built of stone at the cost of $30,000 ($600,000 today) and was outfitted with the most modern equipment. Hilgen exchanged his interest in the grain mill for Trottman's in the woolen mill, renaming it the Hilgen and Wittenberg Woolen Mill, which remained until it was incorporated as the Cedarburg Woolen Mill in 1872. At that time, it was stipulated that executives and supervisors were to be paid the princely sum of $3 a day—for a twelve-hour day.

The original mill consisted of offices and four floors of workspace, not to mention a livery, a blacksmithy, and other outbuildings. A bridge was built at the woolen mill site in 1870 to facilitate the traffic of material between the mill on the west side of the creek and the warehouses on the east side, and aptly renamed Bridge Street. Warehouses and a dye house were constructed across Bridge Street on the south side.

The mill produced top quality yarns, flannels, blankets, socks, and mackinaws. It became one of the very first businesses in America to use catalogues and mail order to sell its merchandise, and shipped as far away as Egypt. The woolen mill later expanded into Grafton to create the only worsted wool (a distinctly different

Woolen Mill workers lined up outside their workplace. It was finished in 1864–1865 to profit from the Union Army's demand for woolen socks and blankets. While the mill missed that business, it prospered in mail order trade, sending Cedarburg products to distant lands. (From the Rappold Collection.)

Hilgen and Company finally prevailed on the railroad barons to run the line out as far as Cedarburg, which served as the northern terminus for some years. This photo shows the Cedarburg railway depot in use after the turn of the century. (From the Rappold Collection.)

weaving process) line west of Philadelphia. William Roebken, another Hilgen relative, supervised the plant.

By employing 150-plus people, women and children included, this industry changed Cedarburg's fate and future, shifting the dynamic from pure agricultural village to part manufacturing town. Its success would breed other factories and lead the way toward a balanced economy that would insulate Cedarburg from the vagaries of the nation's economy. One hundred years later, the woolen mill would again play a vital role in shaping Cedarburg's destiny.

All this time, Father Hilgen had not forgotten his quest to secure rail transportation through his little village. The war's aftermath and the steady growth of Wisconsin as a granary to the world meant steady development of rail lines as well. Yet Cedarburg farmers expressed intense skepticism over any railroad scheme in which they might have to invest. Hilgen sweetened the pot by offering wide swaths of land for a thoroughfare, and finally an intensive community-wide lobbying effort by Hilgen, Horn, and Vogenitz turned the tide when they created a committee to lobby at the state legislature for a railway through Cedarburg.

Those efforts finally paid off when, in May 1870 at Turner Hall, the committee held a formal dinner meeting with the Milwaukee County Board of Supervisors, other prominent citizens, and the press, to discuss creating a stop for Cedarburg on a rail line running north to Fon Du Lac. The party traveled together by carriage up the Green Bay Road, making the trip in roughly three hours. The delegation, being duly impressed with Cedarburg and its environs, and probably as well with the difficulty of traveling on what then passed for roads, determined that the new railroad line would pass through Cedarburg along the path of land Hilgen had years earlier donated.

The Teutonic farm burg on the creek became a manufacturing village on a road of iron.

7. A Teutonic Utopia Realized

By 1900, out of Wisconsin's total population of a little over two million, 709,909 or 34 per cent of its citizens were of German background, and the state's enduring Germanic heritage had been firmly established. German farmers provided a sizable and stable rural population; German cultural societies and institutions such as the musical groups called Liederkranz, the Turnverein, and the Free Thinkers flourished in many communities.
–Richard Zeitlin, Wisconsin State Historical Society

In the year 1900, Cedarburg was 95 percent German. That's right—only five residents in one hundred were *not* of German blood, or put another way, of the 1,738 Cedarburgers on the 1900 census, 87 were non-Teuton. Not even the new German Federal Republic built by Prince Otto von Bismark, Frederick Horn's old schoolmate, could boast so high a percentage of German blood. This new Republic of Germany hosted Hungarians, French, Danes, Belgians, Poles, Gypsies, and Czechoslovaks living within its borders. Not so in Cedarburg, the German Bund by the creek. Hilgen, Boerner, Schroeder, and company had succeeded in creating their Teutonic Burg from raw wilderness. And while they didn't self-consciously go about doing so, they created at the same time a Teutonic Utopia.

Utopian colonies, according to Robert V. Hine, author of *California's Utopian Colonies*, "consist of a group of people who are attempting to establish a new social pattern based upon a vision of the ideal society and who have withdrawn themselves from the community at large to embody that vision in experimental form." These colonies can, by definition, be composed of either religious or secular members; the former stressing (in the Western tradition) a community life inspired by religion, while the latter may express the idealism of a utilitarian creed advantageous to establishing human happiness and a belief in the cooperative way of life.

The Alt Lutheraner Teutons and those enterprising Free Thinkers who gathered around Hilgen and Company sought to create a fully-realized and diversified economy, in which all could prosper and be free to live as they chose. Thus, the mantle of Utopian fit them, although they never saw themselves as such.

Consciously planned utopias sprang up all over America during the time just before and especially after the Civil War. Arriving in the United States, European groups who were persecuted in their own countries hoped to form utopian societies on American soil. Most were agrarian and some were communal in nature, but all sought to keep far from the perceived vices found in the overcrowded cities. While numerous religious and secular utopian experiments dotted the American landscape, the Shakers, the Rappites, the Oneida Community, Brook Farm, and the Amana Colony are perhaps the most famous. However, all but the Amana Colony failed.

New Ulm, Minnesota (the site of the Sioux Uprising that catalyzed the Indian Scare) developed as a planned Teutonic Utopia. The leaders formed a communal land, mill, and business ownership called the Settlement Association, which failed after three years in 1869. The shareholders all lost their money. But the Turn Verein (the social club of these Germans) held sway over the town's destiny for long after, maintaining a German influence in the town that manifested itself for the next century. Even in 1966, a study showed that most of the town's institutions were still in the hands of Turn Verein members, who hired other Turners, who saw to it that only members received contracts to do public works, etc. The authors of the paper noted, ". . . economic pressures, when linked with social will, tend to perpetuate this [German] community, unique in all of ethnic America." Well, not exactly unique.

Evidence of utopia, and a successful one at that, is everywhere to be seen in Cedarburg: the full and prosperous economic life of the inhabitants, the near-universal and vibrant Lutheran worship, the deep respect for the Free

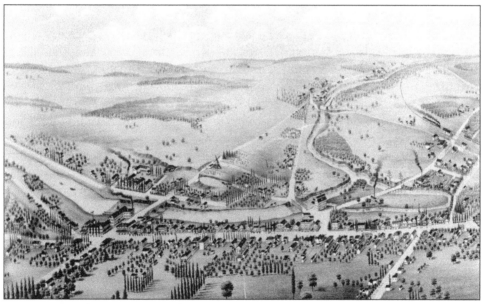

By arranging their economic, religious, and social lives just so, the Teutons who settled Cedarburg created a city that stood as neatly in reality as it did on paper in this lithograph drawn in the late 1870s. In plain view are the gristmill, church steeples, and the woolen mill. (From the Rappold Collection.)

Thinkers' right to worship as they pleased, the dearth of poverty and concomitant absence of illness and disease, the busy and fulfilling social life residents enjoyed, and the highly stable population all compel one to admit that this town was indeed very nearly the perfect place to live. One observer noted that, by bringing to America everything good about life in Germany and leaving the bad behind, settlers achieved an earthly nirvana. He wrote in 1888, "Many . . . live as they did in the old country. They conform to the general laws but keep up their church and family life as they would in Germany."

On October 2, 1873, Fred Horn made a speech to Cedarburg residents summing up the success the village enjoyed:

> Take it all in, there is hardly a county in the state that, for its size, could compare at all with the advantages of Ozaukee County. The land is good, in some parts first rate, with good water everywhere. Water powers not half improved yet, but with plenty of flouring mills, are found in every part; the finest building stone is abundant, and worked to great advantage in quarries near Port Washington, Grafton, and Cedarburg, exhaustless banks of clay for the manufactures of the celebrated Milwaukee brick are to be found. . . . A ready market for these and the product of husbandry can be found at every station of the two competing railroads running parallel through the whole length of the county. . . . As shipping places, we have Port Washington and Milwaukee within a few hour's reach from even the remotest farms.

According to Reverend A.F. Evast, writing in 1889, German farmers taught Americans methods of "rational farming," by rotating crops and the liberal use of fertilizer—a practice summarized in the old German folk sayings, "The manure pit is the farmer's gold pit," and "Where there is manure there is Christ." Above all, the German farmer eschewed speculation, preferring to invest his savings in neighboring fields he was intimately familiar with. Avoiding risks and adventurous experiments necessitating loans, Germans were content to cultivate their small plots intensively, and to progress slowly but steadily towards stability and success. Caring for livestock seems to have been related to German attitudes towards sound farming practices. Settlers who arrived with enough capital soon constructed barns to house their livestock. Johann Kerler expressed the general feeling when he wrote in 1849, "I could not bring myself to leave cattle out in the open during the cold months as the milk would freeze in the cow's udder."

Small wonder that the results of German frugality, careful husbandry, and plain hard work on the Wisconsin landscape were evident by the time of the state census in 1905. At the time, in the townships of Herman and Theresa in Dodge County (an area which had been extremely poor and heavily German in the pioneer era), farms were discovered to have achieved the highest per unit evaluation in the state. By contrast, Yankee townships in the same county, which had led in individual farm valuation for nearly half a century, had declined in value.

"Busy Day" on Washington Ave., Cedarburg, Wis.

This postcard depicts a scene in winter on what was then called Main Street and is now called Washington Avenue. Note the sleighs, the many horses, and the activity on a snowy Market Day. The downtown merchants did a brisk business with the farmers from around the town; most of it was done by barter and little cash traded hands. (From the Robert Armbruster Archive.)

This evidence demonstrated the success of the methodical progress of German agriculturists.

The appeal of this Teutonic approach to the cultivation of land and resources, coupled with the natural bounty of Cedarburg, made the decision to move there a simple one for many Germans. Anyone who spoke German and heard about the land and its people were easily convinced to start farms or businesses and raise families there. Most of the merchants and businessmen who would help create this well-rounded community came in the years between 1850 and 1870, so by 1870, the village's pattern of German settlement was firmly entrenched. The following is a short (and incomplete) list of important German-speaking businessmen who found their way to Cedarburg during the period.

Conrad Wiesler emigrated to the United States in 1851, and in 1876 to Cedarburg, and engaged in the saloon business and farming. At the turn of the twenty-first century a saloon carrying his name exists on the south side of town.

John Weber, who came to Cedarburg in 1855, founded the Cedarburg Brewery with Dr. Fricke and ran it under the firm name of D.T. Fricke & Company until 1864, when he purchased his partner's interest. He enlarged the brewery and added new machinery so that the work was done by steampower. At its height, the brewery employed five men and manufactured 1,500 barrels of beer annually. Weber also recruited musicians and masons from the Black Forest area

Lehmann's Hardware store is pictured here, along with a handful of patrons and employees. Built of rock-faced Niagara Limestone to a height of three stories in 1877, the basement served as a fourth-level storage area. (From the Rappold Collection.)

of Germany to come to Cedarburg, including John Armbruster. Armbruster came to America to play in Weber's Beer Hall Band, and the store he opened in 1884 functioned as both a music store and a jewelry store until the 1950s. Weber later bought the Excelsior Mill (along with the Wurthmann brothers and Fred Kuether) in 1890 and converted it into the Cedarburg Nail Factory.

John Bruss, merchant and later mayor of Cedarburg, was born in the town of Mequon on November 8, 1847, and arrived in Cedarburg in 1868. He owned a general mercantile business, in connection with which he purchased an interest in the hardware business of H.G. Groth in 1880. Mr. Bruss married the boss's daughter, a prevalent pattern in Cedarburg.

Henry Hentschel was born in Fischheim, Saxony, on April 29, 1839, and came to the United States in 1860. That same year, he purchased an interest in the mercantile business of Bodendorfer & Company in the Hamilton district. He took on a partner, L.E. Jochem, and changed the firm's name to Hentschel & Jochem in 1868. Nine years later, the pair moved the business to Cedarburg.

L.E. Jochem was born in Mequon in 1853. His parents, Adam and Gertrude Jochem, were natives of Germany who came to the United States and settled in the town of Mequon in 1840, and therefore were among the earliest settlers of Ozaukee County. Jochem would act as agent for the American Express Company and as deputy postmaster and postmaster from the store in the center of town. He married Mary Bodendorfer in 1878, who just so happened to be the daughter of the man whose firm he had joined after it was sold to Hentschel.

C.W. Lehmann came to Cedarburg in 1867 to start a hardware store, and the following year took in his brother Julius Lehmann to create the store Lehmann Brothers. They erected a three-story stone building almost in the center of town in 1874. The first floor of the entire building was used as a store and workshop, the second floor as a dwelling, and the third was a hall occupied as a lodge room by a communal society.

William Vogenitz was born near Magdeburg, Prussia, in the year 1820. He emigrated to the United States in 1839 and first settled in the town of Mequon, but starting in the spring of 1840, he spent eight years searching the area for a place where he could settle and prosper. The search concluded in Cedarburg, where he opened a store and was engaged in the mercantile business until 1866. He then became the justice of the peace, a post he held for over 25 years. Vogenitz also served in the Assembly of 1856, was county clerk of old Washington Company, was a member of the town board, and worked as secretary of the Cedarburg Mutual Fire Insurance Company.

Alongside these men, Father Hilgen and Company continued developing enterprises left and right. In 1868 Hilgen built a soda water factory called "Cold Springs" to capitalize on the Hilgen Spring Park, a place becoming so famous that articles in both English and German-speaking newspapers were written about it all over the Midwest. One newspaper account told of visitors flocking to the resort from as far away as St. Louis and New Orleans to absorb and bask in its waters. According to the Ozaukee County Historical Society's newsletter:

> Hilgen Spring Park was quite renowned. It was a summer resort and Chicago families came there to spend the summer. They had a hotel, a rathskeller, nine pin alleys, bathhouses, spring fed pond with fish, and an artesian spring fountain. There was also a band stand, a dance hall, a boat landing with a number of row boats with an attendant, and for 25 cents you could row up and down the unpolluted water.
>
> It was also the focus of the burghers' social life on summery Saturdays. They would come to absorb beer and swap tales in the cool basement tap room until about 5:00 when the steam would whistle in the boiler rooms to signal that their hot baths in the huge metal tub were ready.

Ever the promoter, Hilgen took the lead in developing the easy transportation that would feed his resort with regular customers. He had been the first to offer money and land to the Milwaukee and Northern Railroad in 1870, and now he wanted to continue developing the line. Father Hilgen financed and oversaw the erection of a railroad depot, which for a time was the northernmost point of the line. The depot had a turntable at Portland and Hamilton Roads where engines could be turned back around in the other direction. Hilgen's daughters cleaned and swept the cars each night before the return journey to Milwaukee.

The railroad contributed to a boomlet—in 1878 there were 1,200 residents, up 20 percent from the 1870 census. The local farmers were urged to open land to development to meet the need for housing, and in 1883 the *Cedarburg News* noted that while there was not a single home available for rent, 15 homes were being built. In the same year, there were four trains going north and south daily, bringing salesmen and peddlers (and causing the authorities to later legislate against magazine peddlers, etc.) who would set up their wares right on the sidewalk. The city also boasted six hotels numbering well over 100 rooms.

In 1868, Hilgen formed a bank with $25,000 raised in $100 shares bought by Hilgen, Henry Weyhausen, William Schroeder, Friedrich Schatz, Juergen Schroeder, Joseph Trottman, and Adolf Zimmerman. The bank soon closed, yet all involved were able to salvage their full shares. Hilgen said only, "The time is not yet ripe for an independent bank in Cedarburg."

As mentioned previously, in 1872 Hilgen and Schroeder built the Hilgen Manufacturing Company, a milling and planing factory that produced mouldings, windows, doors, and other wood products for residential and business construction. Located where the current American Legion Post sits, the business was phenomenally successful, with a warehouse in Milwaukee opening a few years later. Hilgen Manufacturing eventually supplied the windows, sashes, moldings, and doors for many major institutional buildings constructed in the Milwaukee area.

In 1896, the Hilgen's and Wittenberg's woolen mill needed to expand once again, and with the creek flow insufficient to meet their needs, they invested in a steam generator heated by cord wood supplied by local farmers. A 1893 drawing shows 12 buildings in the complex, including the mill, warehouses, coach house,

The railroad depot, now on Pioneer Village property north of Cedarburg, was built by Frederick Hilgen to facilitate Hilgen Spring Park visitors' travel to and from Cedarburg. Farmers also found it convenient as a way to deliver grains to market. Being that this was the terminus of the line for some years, just beyond the station sat a "lazy susan" on which the engines and cars could be turned about. (From the Rappold Collection.)

shipping, store, offices, a bleach house, and a dye shed. In the main factory carding, weaving, spinning, and knitting machine operations were carried out on the three floors above ground. Washing and finishing was done in the basement, which was connected by a tunnel to the dye shed across Bridge Street. It rapidly became the most active woolen mill in the Midwest, employing between 80 and 100 men and women.

In 1897, the mill again led the town into a new age by installing the first electrical generator, providing lights to the mill and to three Wittenberg homes nearby (Diedrich's brick house across the way was also heated by steam from the factory piped in by a tunnel used by Diedrich in the winter and sloppy spring months to commute).

Father Hilgen had driven the town to prosperity by sheer force of will and creative spirit. Many other areas of the country were equally blessed with bounteous natural resources, but few wrested such solid and stable livings for themselves and their descendants from the bounty. Hilgen brought a vision of a German island of civilization to the wild forest and worked enthusiastically to make sure the dream came true. He and the town certainly reaped the benefits of his effervescence and far-sightedness. Upon Father Hilgen's death on March 27, 1879, as the *History of Washington and Ozaukee Counties, Wisconsin* put it, his passing "was deeply deplored by the community in which he lived, and when the imposing obsequies giving back his remains to mother earth had ended, scarcely a heart in all the town of Cedarburg but mourned the loss . . ."

Hilgen had always invested and reinvested heavily in every venture he could, if only to give the community confidence in its viability. Consequently, at his death his widow Louisa and the executor of the estate, president of Hilgen Manufacturing, John Winner, spent the next five years unraveling his ventures and finding everything heavily mortgaged—even the furniture. The estate stood deeply in debt, and if creditors pressed their claims too quickly it would collapse. After Hilgen's death, there were two attempts to sell or auction the Park and both failed. His son Fred subsequently took it over in 1878.

Other mills and businesses sprung up and prospered in the years 1870–1900. Around 1871, H. Wehausen Company built a stone mill four stories tall, called Excelsior Mill, just east of Columbia Mill and between Cedarburg and Grafton. John S. Weber, the brewer, bought it in 1890 and organized the Cedarburg Nail and Wire Factory, along with E.G. Wurthmann and others. The creek's original 25-foot drop at that spot provided the best waterpower in the area, as the 100 foot millrace provided the equivalent of 175 horsepower. Wurthmann went to New York in 1890 to study the new round nail technology and returned with nine machines that could turn wire into nail. Thus, the state-of-the-art Cedarburg Nail Factory became the first in Wisconsin to make round nails.

In 1872, a windmill was also built in town 1872 at Bridge Street east of the creek, high on a hill. Created by pioneers named Deauvel, Ascher, and Spiller, the chief product was Pearl Barley, a favorite among Germans who used it for soups and sausage filler. The trio tried to develop a market for Pearl Barley, but it never

This windmill, clearly visible on the lithograph beginning this chapter, stood atop the highest point in Cedarburg just feet from the creek. The cemetery that is visible behind it still exists on the hill at Bridge Street. (From the Rappold Collection.)

became commonly used in America with the exception of local housewives and butchers. After ten years, they sold to Henry Thiel, who ran it for five years before it burned down, leaving only a stone base. That was dismantled later because the community felt it was a danger to children who played in and around it.

Situated for a time due north of Cedarburg just past the Covered Bridge, the ghost town of Kaehler's Mills contained two mills (saw and grist), a post office, general store, smithy, and several shops in the 1870s. It, along with Hamilton, suffered a slow death after the railroad went through Cedarburg. The people of Kaehler's Mills, however, caused the historic covered bridge to be built. The bridge was constructed in Baraboo and brought to Cedarburg in 1876. It was originally called the "Red Bridge" and spanned 120 feet in length by 12 feet in width. Made of a pine peculiar to Baraboo, the planks and timber were cut there and shipped to Cedarburg to be assembled. The type of construction is called lattice truss, with interlacing 3-foot by 10-foot planks held together by 2-inch hardwood pins and floored with 3-inch floor planking.

Speculation runs rampant as to why certain bridges of the time were covered, from suggestions that they were welcome shelter for rain-soaked travelers, to protection from Indian attacks. Another theory is that the covering blocked oxen's and horses' line of site, keeping them from balking at crossing the rapidly flowing stream. Others suggest, in what is the most likely explanation, that the cover kept the surface free from snow, ice, and in summer, slick rain. They point out that a cover would delay any inevitable rot that would set in with untreated green wood. A few, however, claim the covering was added just because it looked nice and could be seen from afar. Whatever the explanation, it still exists and looks beautiful, and no oxen have resisted crossing for quite some time. The bridge officially ended its career in 1961 and was made a landmark with the county creating a park around it.

Besides the commercial and business development, the society developed in ways peculiar to the area and culture during this time. In *Contented Among Strangers,* Linda Pickle writes that German-Americans preferred to marry within their own ethnic group after coming to America, a practice called "endogamy." Religious affiliation, especially the strict dogmatic tendencies of Lutheran sects, fueled endogamy by encouraging marriage within the congregation, creating eventually what could be called be a community of cousins. Cedarburg developed a similar tradition of endogamous marriage, and any glance at two or three local genealogies show that intermarriage was rife in the town.

This "tribal" practice of intermarriage rooted German tradition to the soil from where they took place, resulting in practices and celebrations characterizing much of life in Midwestern rural and suburban America, even today. German traditions such as St. Nicholas Day, not lighting or decorating the Christmas tree until Christmas Eve, and caroling are closely associated with Christmas all over the country in even non-German homes.

The last covered bridge in Wisconsin sits a couple miles north of Cedarburg. Retired in 1962 after a concrete and steel structure replaced it, this bridge was made entirely of wood, including the 2-inch dowels that hold the planks together.

Some non-holiday German/Lutheran traditions, although more obscure, live on today in the smaller towns. One such example is ringing the church bell for the dead and another includes serving afternoon coffee and a snack, or preparing homemade foods. Likewise, Saturday night dances and potlucks still personify the rural life, while another centers around singing German hymns ("Onward Christian Soldiers," "Silent Night," etc.) even in Methodist or Baptist churches.

As a consequence this "tradition seepage," residents of the Midwest have come to recognize central Teutonic characteristics as indistinguishable from Midwestern values. Pickle states Germans showed:

> conservatism, thrift, self-reliance, industriousness, cleanliness, and success and skill as farmers, homemakers, and craftspeople. They display a consciousness of and pride in their heritage that seems to go beyond a mere nostalgic cultural loyalty. Their deep rooted, family-based stability on the land and in the locality is the core of the [Midwesterner's] self-awareness.

Central to the lives of citizens in this new land was, of course, church. The town had three vital Lutheran congregations, First Immanuel, Trinity, and Immanuel, and one large Catholic congregation, St. Francis Borgia, at the turn of the century. Each had its beginnings in the very first years of settlement, growing steadily into stable and strong institutions that still thrive.

Trinity Lutheran Church formed around congregants from Pomerania, led to America by Pastor Kindermann, who left some of the congregation in Lebanon (near Watertown) and some in Cedarburg, while he accompanied those who went to Kirchayn. On land donated by Ludwig Groth and his brother-in-law Frederick Dobberpuhl, the church built its first log parish at Evergreen Boulevard and Western Avenue, with the cemetery by its side forming what is now Founders Park. They moved the cemetery, which was difficult to utilize because the limestone extended to nearly the grass, to Zur Ruhe in 1868. This land was donated to the church by the teacher and organist Johannes Kuehn.

It was in 1844 that the parishioners created the first schools for children. Classes were taught by the pastor and Kuehn in Lutheran catechism, reading, and arithmetic during the day in the church building. Kuehn was paid 18¢ a month per child, 25¢ for playing the organ at any service not deemed regular worshipping, and $20 a year for cleaning and heating the structure. The children were given eight weeks of vacation: two weeks during each haying season and four during harvest.

In 1864, the congregation built another stone school on the west side of Washington and north of Columbia (next to where Hoffman's Meat Market now does business) where all the children from town, whether they were members of Trinity or not, attended. The school operated until 1932. The present church was built on the east side of the Creek of Columbia Road in 1890.

In this scene from high atop St. Francis Borgia Church on the south end of town, one can make out the steeples of the three main Lutheran churches of the day. Immediately in the foreground stands Immanuel, peeking out over the top of the mill is Trinity, and on the left beyond the tall school building stands First Immanuel. These churches were the center of religious and Teutonic cultural life for Cedarburgers. (From the Rappold Collection.)

St. Francis Borgia formed in late 1842 when Father Martin Kundig held a service for Irish Catholics in the home of Irish settler Humphrey Desmond, and later a log church was constructed nearby. This was replaced by a frame one in 1852, and then the present structure was built in 1870. The land cost $1,686, the church (made of Bedford limestone) came in at $30,000, much of which came from Irish congregants who still lived in the area. They mostly inhabited Mequon, as around this time the Irish were leaving Cedarburg to the Germans.

Immanuel Lutheran Church was formed in the first days of the settlement by seven men: Frederick Lange, Christieb Hennig, Johannes Wirth, Christian Geier, Johannes Groth, Carl Schueler, and Joseph Schaub. The congregation, at this point called simply Immanuel, grew immensely and moved to a 48-foot by 22-foot building vacated by another small congregation whose liberality sealed its doom, the Humanhtzngemude [human congregation] in 1858. The charismatic conservative Reverend F.A. Ahner led the congregation.

Ahner preached dictatorially, accusing many of the congregation of behavior unbecoming a Lutheran. Mutinous members demanded Ahner's expulsion and possession of the church's property. However, an investigation by the Synod found no wrongdoing by Ahner and reaffirmed his legal possession of the property. Yet membership, unhappy with the finding, declared they would no longer recognize Ahner as their pastor and held possession of the church. Finally, after negotiations, the mutineers bought out the small pro-Ahner faction for the sum of $349 in 1862. This tiny congregation named itself First Immanuel, laying claim to primacy by way of its name. Ahner bailed out of the whole mess by accepting a "call" to another church in Michigan less than a year later. There is no word from Michigan of any more church mutinies lying in his wake.

Whether because of their high standards of Lutheran worship or their reputation for disputation, First Immanuel had considerable trouble finding a leader for their parish, sharing a pastor with neighboring congregations until 1879 when they hired their own. He lasted ten years before leaving the elders to again search for a shepherd. This time they had the good fortune of stumbling upon Paul Weichmann, the "Building Pastor," who was responsible for introducing the English language into the school's curriculum, hiring the first full-time teacher, and building the stone church in 1891 at a cost of less than $5,000.

Immanuel, for its pastor, turned to Reverend Habel of the Star of David congregation in Kirchayn to lead them in the wake of their troubles. Except for a six-year break, Habel would lead them until 1873, when they found and called upon Reverend E.G. Strassburger, who served Immanuel for 46 years. Immanuel's stone church on Washington Avenue was built in 1882 by Vollmar and Weber; a school was built on Western in 1896. A cemetery was added on Jefferson and Bridge Streets in 1890.

While church activities within their parish made up the core of each congregation member's social and cultural life, another important element, the Turn Verein, became the actual fulcrum on which Cedarburg's social life turned. First organized in 1853 in Hamilton, the Turn Verein in Cedarburg sprang from the Teutonic Turner Movement founded by Prussian Friederich Jahn. In 1812, he initiated a secular program combining physical fitness with the ideals of free citizenship. Jahn wrote, "The education of the people aims to realize the ideal of an all-around human being, citizen, and member of society in each individual; gymnastics are one means toward a complete education of the people."

In Europe, the Metternich Regime saw Turners as a danger to the government, thus repressing them beginning in 1819. That move had the usual result of making the movement's ideals flourish in people's minds, especially in America where such political beliefs were enshrined in the Constitution. The Turnerbund was transplanted to America early, along with its fundamental purposes of making people strong in mind, body, and morals, achieving harmonious education as an essential prerequisite to perfecting and preserving democracy, and furthering the intellectual and moral welfare of both children and adults by maintaining libraries, reading rooms, lectures, and debates on governance and civil liberties. The Cedarburg Turn Verein organized in August 1853 as the Cedar and Hamilton Society, starting with 45 members.

Free Thinking societies were often closely associated with the Turners, especially in the period before 1890. Free Thinkers, or *Freie Gemeinden*, opposed religious authoritarianism of both the Protestant and Catholic churches, upholding doctrines of rationalism, science, and humanism while contributing significantly to the growth of religious and social liberalism. Congregations of

Free Thinkers were widespread in pioneer Wisconsin. In 1852, for instance, there were 31 Free-thinking congregations, mostly in small towns near German settlements in the eastern part of the state. Other more radical or socialist German groups associated with Free Thinkers and at times participated with the Turners in community events. In 1876, the Milwaukee German Union of Radicals, for example, called upon "lovers of free thinking" to join them in "the name of freedom, justice, and the general welfare." On another occasion, radicals joined Free Thinkers and Turners in celebrating Thomas Paine's birthday. Socialist meetings often took place in Turner halls while German workers formed reading and culture clubs "to improve their education and knowledge through . . . the exchange of opinions in the field of social reforms."

The Cedarburg Turners built their hall in the center of town in 1868. Adlai Horn, grandson of Frederick, comments in a 1940 *Cedarburg News* article:

> The word "Turn" means gymnastics, and if you read the early history of the Turn Verein in Germany, they were subject to criticism in that it was alleged that they paid more attention to their bodies than their souls, for it was primarily a physical culture thing, a strength through joy proposition, and many of the leaders belonged to the Free Thinkers, who were skeptical of religion and the church, and were branded as agnostics. We kids loved to go to the Turn Schule. They had classes for children, teenagers and adults, men and women, and we learned the difficult gymnastic exercises, such as performed on what was called

Turner Hall saw many community theater productions, church events, school plays, and traveling minstrel shows performed on its stage. This production of the "Womanless Wedding" actually took place in the next century, but the central location and stone construction of Turner Hall meant that it would be used for almost 100 years. (From the Rappold Collection.)

horses and on parallel bars. The people at the time enjoyed the theater and Turner Hall had a very fine stage and scenery, and was used by many dramatic groups, all home talent, and a number of the plays were all German and well attended.

In every Turner Hall were painted the following words summing up the Turner philosophy of vitality in all things: *frisch, fromm, froh, frei.* Or in English: fresh, pious, happy, free.

Turner Hall was also used for balls. Although "work is what Germans do," as represented in this old saying, "Die Arbeit Macht das Leben Suess," or "Work Makes Life Sweet," dancing could be said to be what Germans did after work. Any occasion gave excuse to dance: the Fourth of July, Thanksgiving, Easter, Christmas, New Year, and almost any other reason the town could create for kicking up its heels, such as the Masked Ball, transformed Turner Hall into a ballroom. It had a dining and kitchen area, a dance floor, and a large bar. The hall also contained a room on the second floor where city fathers would meet, acting somewhat like a pseudo council chambers, as well as a small jail in the basement. These balls and entertainments gave the well-to-do, upper-crust women who enjoyed wearing lavish jewelry and fine clothes a chance to do so. Mrs. Hilgen especially became known for her Irish Black Lace caps. She not only loved music, dancing, and dressing in the finest attire, she enjoyed viewing the many productions at Turner Halle. She wrote in 1882 to her daughter Emma:

> Our children's theater was very good, they did not make any mistakes. The stage was full with very small girls and boys and they sang beautifully. The older ones recited [sic] and performed, they had the best suits from Milwaukee. Albert Johan [Boerner] was the Prince, Emma Hueter was Cinderella, then we celebrated the wedding. The Turn Halle was never so crowded as it was yesterday evening, upstairs and downstairs were completely full, they performed until 12 o'clock and danced until 4 o'clock, many friends were there and everybody had a good time.

The schools used the gymnasium for physical education classes, a very German contribution to public school education in this country. All the high school plays, wrestling matches, basketball games, grade school productions, women's club plays, band concerts, European artists variety shows, barn dance shows, apple grower exhibits, farm equipment shows, garden club shows, Wisconsin Symphony Orchestra visits, Wirth and Armbruster demonstrations of new products, etc. took place there. As one can probably guess, Turner Hall was in almost constant use.

The Turners also acted as a benevolent society, stepping in with cash to support families who fell prey to the vagaries of life and helping to nurture other social institutions and activities like libraries and sponsoring picnics. Members donated a dime every month to the coffers of the Turner Society, creating a large surplus used to support worthy causes.

The churches and the Turn Verein show how vitally important it was for immigrants to create familiar institutions in America, to develop a mini-Bund in the American wilderness. This tendency to build institutions that mirrored Teutonic examples may have been an attempt to put off assimilation, but instead had the effect of easing their movement into the American mainstream. David Bowers wrote in the *Foreign Influences in American Life*:

> In rural areas which are sparsely settled and where the new immigrant is rarely thrown into highly intimate association with the native born, there is less need or occasion for adjustment and greater opportunity for retaining old customs. The result is a less intense form of conflict, but a more protracted one. Groups differences [*sic*] under such circumstances will remain submerged and therefore less inciting, but they will continue to exist.

Clearly the immigrant farmers in Cedarburg replicated social and cultural institutions of their Fatherland to feel more at home. In *Immigration: Cultural Conflicts and Social Adjustments*, Lawrence Brown described:

These Cedarburg Turners turn a trick for the camera. The Turn Verein faced challenges in German principalities because they were seen as secular threats to a religion-based governance. Yesterday's secular humanists, they were often closely connected to the Free Thinkers, or Teutonic Deists. Physical exercise was an integral aspect of the Turner attempt to educate the "mind, body, and spirit." (From the Robert Armbruster Archive.)

the more artifacts, modes of living, and traditional elements an immigrant can bring along with him, the better he will accommodate himself to his new environment and situation—His church, his coffee-house, his tavern, his fraternal organizations, all facilitate a ready adjustment. If he could not live with his countrymen in an environmental replica of his own customs, habits and traditions . . . the result would be social upheaval and personal demoralization.

Yet American institutions began to intrude ever so gently. The first public school was started soon after the state mandated that a "free school" be operated in every township in 1854. First located in a brick and frame building on Washington Avenue where Advent Church now stands, it then moved across the street a few years later. The first principal, P.K. Gannon, served until 1875. By 1893, it became clear the town was outgrowing the school, and after much discussion and one vote against, the building committee and the school board financed a new school with $18,500.

The resulting Lincoln building was constructed by Vollmar and Company with woodwork done by A. Knuppel at a cost of $17,976. Once it was finished in 1894, the first floor of the old school was used by the fire department and the second floor by sixth and seventh grade classes. In 1894, there were 251 children in five grades attending the school. High school came to Cedarburg in 1896 when a three-year curriculum was added as secondary education. Orange and black

This postcard (c. 1909) shows the Lincoln Grade School building to the left and the newly constructed high school (now called the Washington Building). Three stories with bell tower, the Greek Revival/Gothic structure built with Niagara Limestone dominates the town center skyline. (Courtesy of the Robert Armbruster Archive.)

The Cedarburg Volunteer Fire Department's running team is shown here with the hose they would run to the fires with. Notice that instead of a Dalmatian, they had a Dachshund as companion. (From the Rappold Collection.)

became the class colors, a tradition that continues unabated. The school each year, on a Sunday in July near the beginning of the six-week summer vacation, held a picnic at Hilgen's Resort.

The County Fair, held in September nearer harvest time, sponsored a Children's Day where kids were let out of school and into the fair for free. On other fair days, schoolmasters organized spelling bees and Declamatory Contests. Sporting events, such as dog and horse racing, were popular and firemen had picnics dating back to their inception. All of these took place at Fairground Park (later named Fireman's Park). Children in the summer swam only in the millraces when the water was low since the creek was full of sewage from all the outhouses built out over it, as well as with industrial run-off from the mills.

Another institution established at the time would become an important cog in the village's development, the Cedarburg Volunteer Fire Department (CFD). The first fire company was organized in March 1867, had 31 members partake in its inauguration, and used a hand engine and about 500 feet of leather hose to do battle with blazes. Soon afterward it merged with the Turner Society, but in 1875, the state served notice that a new fire station must be built, and CFD separated from the Turners and subsequently constructed a station in the fall. As prepared as they were, records from that year show there hadn't been a fire for two years. In 1894, the station moved to the vacated schoolhouse, operating there for 14 years until it burned to the ground in Cedarburg's most spectacular fire.

In 1885, the City of Cedarburg was incorporated and the Cedarburg Police Department was established. The justice of the peace used a small room in the basement of Turner Hall for a jail, and mainly locked up strangers for minor indiscretions after imbibing too much at a local tavern. They were given bread and water for breakfast and sent on their way.

The first mayor, Fred Horn, wrote and oversaw the execution of the following laws soon after Cedarburg became an official city. The laws themselves and the order in which they were passed tells us something about the town's residents and their concerns. Written and passed on:

April 21: "It will be illegal to commit disorderly conduct, vagrancy, drunkenness, gambling, disturbing the peace, prostitution, assault, and indecent exposure." On the same day it was made illegal to conduct a circus or any other gathering where the sale of goods took place, except the monthly Farmers' Market Day. The third decree they passed, again the same day, was against the running wild of livestock within the city limits. A fourth regulated the sale of liquor.

April 25: A measure passed regulating "hawkers" or "peddlers" on city sidewalks.

May 23: The sixth of the city's laws created a dog license ordinance at $1 a dog.

May 25: The Slops Law passed. No slops or rubbish were to be thrown on the streets or sidewalks.

The final set of laws to be framed and passed in that first year included an October ordinance compelling all in the city limits to assist putting out fires and another instituting parking restrictions, where "no horse or carriage shall be left to stand in the street or on sidewalks for more than two hours." The city also legislated against storing firewood, or anything else for that matter, on city sidewalks for more than 48 hours. Another measure prevented individuals from digging ditches or otherwise changing the roadbeds. The sidewalk laws must have been sorely needed, especially by the ladies in the town, as one decision mandated that no horse or cow were to be led over the (then) wooden walks.

The city could communicate by telegraph, an improvement that might have helped avoid the wholesale panic caused by the Indian Scare. The first office resided in the new train station in 1870 until a new one was built in 1907. The telegraph agents stood in a bottleneck of information since they were the only people able to interpret Morse code used in communicating messages over the lines. They took all messages from the outside world, translated the dots and dashes into written English, and passed them along by messenger boy. These couriers ran the streets of Cedarburg regularly, running postcards with notes from household to household, or from housewife to businessman. Many postcards from the time, some with photos or lithographs of Cedarburg and its surroundings, survive today.

The telephone, invented in 1876 and first marketed in 1880, first appeared in town as a public phone in the Boerner Brothers Store in 1883. From there, one could call any of the several dozen phones in stores in Milwaukee, for a price. By the end of that year, there were 11 phones in Cedarburg, mostly installed in businesses: Cedarburg Woolen Mills, Hentschel & Jochem Store, Boerner Brothers, Hilgen Manufacturing Company, Milwaukee & Northern Railroad Depot, B.J. VonVolkenberg Company, Charles Gottschalk Livery, A. Bodendorfer, Jacob Zaun, John Bruss, and Dr. Mayer. By 1900, there were many phones on "farmer," or party, lines.

After the phone exchange went in, the operator told Adlai Horn's mother in his presence that, "If you only knew how many Cedarburg businessmen called up different women. I know, but I won't tell." Horn's mother asked if her husband Alexander was also guilty. "So far not" was the operator's response.

The *Cedarburg News* debuted in 1882 as a political platform for Fred Horn. He wrote all the copy and his son Alexander, who learned the newspaper business at the *Milwaukee Sentinel*, ran the presses. He took over after his father's death in 1892 and the paper remained in Horn family hands for over a century when it was finally sold to Jim Conley in 1988.

An ad appearing in the *Cedarburg News* on March 14, 1883 gives us a glimpse of the times for working people in the Burg:

> Wanted: strong capable woman to do general housework and work part of each day in the cheese factory. Three dollars per week [roughly 5.5¢ per hour] will be paid to one who suits and proves herself competent. Apply at the cheese factory, near the Cedarburg Railroad Depot.

These women, either coming from or going to church, would have looked forward to the afternoon in the outdoors at Hilgen Spring Park or in their own yard sharing good food, beer, conversation, and music with friends and family. German Sundays, however, came under attack in the state by Yankee Puritans who sought to make the Sabbath a day of rest and quiet, not Gemeutlichkeit. (From the Rappold Collection.)

Blending the Teutonic Utopia with an American system was not altogether easy or seamlessly accomplished. In her doctoral paper *The Americanization of German Immigrants: Language, Religion, and Schools in Nineteenth Century Wisconsin*, Susan Kuyper notes that cultural threats cast a pall over the otherwise idyllic quality of the Teutonic Bund created in Cedarburg. Two main threats came from sharp disagreement between the Yankee ideas of temperance and sabbatarianism and "German Sundays" and the desire of German speakers to see their children educated in the language of the homeland.

In 1872, the state legislature passed the Graham Liquor Law, "An Act to provide against the evils resulting from the sale of intoxicating liquors," which took direct aim at "German Sundays," the Teutons' practice of after-church dancing and drinking parties. In 1889, the Bennett Law threatened German denominational schools by requiring certain courses be taught in English. In both cases, the laws were prompted by powerful Yankee (and often Republican) fears that assimilation of the (predominantly Democrat) German population was failing. Another measure, closely connected to the Graham Law, made it illegal to "sell, barter, or give away" intoxicating liquors on Sunday. None of these laws were ever enforced in the Teutonic Bund of Cedarburg, which had a way of ignoring anything unpleasant or contrary to its citizens' wishes. In 1872, Reverend W.E. Armitage presented the Teutonic side of "German Sunday":

> At home have their beer gardens, private establishments, and also palace gardens and such places as public parks where no beer is sold, no amusements provided, nothing but the heightened beauties of nature and convenient seats and look-out places, and so on to enable all to enjoy them. It is not their way to leave home and go to entertainments to which they cannot take their wives and children.

In June 1890, the mostly German-speaking political elite held a anti-Bennett Law political convention to protest the attack on German-speaking schools. Consequently, the Bennett Law seemed the only issue of consequence in elections that year. Wisconsin's eastern counties and the populace, voting in higher numbers than ever before, gave the Democrats a clean sweep of state and county offices. The law was repealed in 1892.

In matters great and small, the period from 1870 to 1900 demonstrated that an ethnic and language group could relocate to virgin land and create a vibrant and vital community. The Alt Lutherans found their way to the wooded shores of Cedar Creek and wrested a clearing in the forest where they worshiped, built, farmed, and lived as they chose. The Teutonic Utopia Father Hilgen had dreamed of now existed and the community had begun to, and would continue to through the first part of the new century, set the record of its existence in stone.

8. The Gilded-German Age Gives Way to the American Century

Germans in America between 1855 and 1915 lived not in the United States, but in German-America, and lived and wrote for German-America, in very many cases, rather than for the United States of America. The World War, with its hatreds and persecutions, its propaganda and coercion, shook the hyphen loose from its moorings and ended the German-American era which had lasted so long.

–John Hawgood in The Tragedy of German-America

The second generation of Cedarburg residents greeted the dawn of a new century amidst booming times. Businesses prospered while the population stabilized, institutions thrived, and the farms burst with bounty. The bustling burg acted as the spoke of Ozaukee County's trading wheel, but it also lay just off the beaten path of the Green Bay Road, a main highway along the lakeshore. And so Cedarburg found itself in splendid semi-isolation within an hour's train ride of a major metropolis. This not only meant that the outside world was within easy reach for the residents of the town, but also that that world, if it wished to intrude upon Cedarburg, would have to make a conscious effort to do so.

It did.

The turn of the twentieth century, called the American Century by many historians, swept into Cedarburg with all the brash brilliance and technological titillation of the time. The Gilded Age took over from the Victorian Age and introduced a purely American society in the decades before and immediately after 1900. Society would never be the same; the lives of workers and housewives alike changed inalterably. Driven by automobiles, tractors, telephones, electricity, and household products, the twentieth century would compel these Teutonic farmers, industrialists, and merchants to be assimilated into the American Dream. But not before leaving their German imprint on the landscape.

As noted in the last chapter, Father Hilgen died in 1878, leaving a thriving set of enterprises for his many children to operate. The other half of Hilgen and

This photo shows carriages and buggies, all horse-drawn, before the turn of the century. Within a few years the city's streets would be lined with automobiles and trucks. The skyline would boast telephone and electric wiring, and English would be spoken on those lines. (From the Rappold Collection.)

Company, Frederick Boerner, died only months later, survived by eight children and his widow Anna, or "Oma." Oma would look after the young clan (the eldest son Arthur was but 20 years old) and would ride herd over the vast and disparate Boerner enterprises well into the new century. Now called Boerner Brothers, Boerner's general merchandise store was easily the largest of the general stores in the county and certainly the one with the best selection of goods.

Yet size and aggressive advertising—their motto was "Cheapest Cash Store in the County"—failed to make for an instant success during the youths' watch, and the store struggled. Arthur, who had left for New York to study medicine in 1879, returned home after less than a year to get the store back on course, abandoning his plans to become a doctor. Eventually, Arthur and his brethren made the store a success and even began something that would soon become a cultural phenomenon across America—the chain store—adding outlets in Port Washington and West Bend. That foray into Gilded Age commerce, however, ultimately failed to inoculate the family's fortunes against the vagaries of a new American economy. The new ideas and ideals of American culture invaded every corner of even this Teutonic land, replacing much of the Old World influence, even as Germanism influenced the American Midwest.

The Boerner family story best exemplifies Cedarburg's changing fortunes during the period. In the 1890s, both America and Cedarburg experienced a rapid change from agricultural base to an industrial one, and the Boerners went along for the ride. They aggressively developed industry within the town just as their father had done. By 1894, the store was so prosperous, Arthur's family took an extended trip to Europe to visit relatives. Upon returning and flush with confidence, he began Boerner Brothers Company (later Boerner Brothers

106

Manufacturing Association). In partnership with his brothers, this new venture invested in many enterprises such as a creamery, shoe, and furniture factories, and a northern Wisconsin iron/manganese mine.

Riding the wave of technological innovation and the new American consumerism, in 1899, Arthur installed what he called his "waterworks" in the family's homestead, Cedar Hedge Farm. The indoor plumbing and running water so impressed neighbors that, at a birthday party soon after installation, wondering children pulled the chain so many times that it overflowed, much to the maid's consternation and the kids' giggling delight.

The Boerners lived in Victorian splendor, employing several to assist in running the house. They kept a hired girl at $3 per week plus room and board, and also a *kindermadchen* (nanny) for the smallest children at $1.50-plus. They even owned one of the first autos in Cedarburg, an Oldsmobile "two-seater in which the back of the front seat also served as the back of the rear seat so that those in the front seat could see where they were going and those in the back seat could see where they'd been," according to a Boerner biographer.

Running a household as large as Cedar Hedge was quite a feat, and Oma deserved all the credit, according to family histories. Her glue bound the disparate interests of sons and daughters to the family's roots on Cedar Hedge. The glue was so effective that the Boerner grandchildren, some of whom attained great fame and stature in other parts of the country, saw Oma and Cedar Hedge as their touchstone, losing touch with Cedarburg only after her death in 1922.

Household chores for the rest of the population of Cedarburg differed not in volume from Mrs. Boerner's, but in workload. They lacked the extra hired help and spent long hours performing considerable tasks. This from *Victorian Age Housekeeping*, a Victorian era web site put up by historian Melissa Kalson:

> Monday usually meant laundry. Soaking had usually been started well ahead, as early as Saturday night for those whose religious beliefs forbade any sort of labor on Sunday. On Monday morning, each load of wash was wrung, put through two washings where stubborn dirt was rubbed out on a corrugated board, then boiled for twenty minutes in a third tub of soapy water before being transferred with a wooden "fork" to a cold rinse.
>
> After a final rinse in water lightly tinged with bluing, the laundry was wrung out again and hung to dry. Items to be starched first were put aside to be dipped in and rubbed with a solution so hot that hands were continually plunged into cold water to prevent scalding. With clean, wet clothes hanging from the lines, lunch could be set out. Monday meals were planned to involve as little preparation and attention as possible. Leftovers would do, or something roasted in the oven along with baked potatoes or macaroni, a canned vegetable and an easily prepared dessert, such as baked apples. This left time in the afternoon to scrub porches and laundry area with leftover wash water. By the time the family sat down to their evening meal, all traces of the day's work would be stored

107

Cedarburg loved parades and especially the July Fourth Parade. This scene shows the patriotic procession of automobiles that made up much of the 1908 July Fourth parade contingent. (From the Rappold Collection.)

away for another week, and the clean laundry sprinkled and rolled in cloth for ironing the next day.

One day a week was set aside for a general household cleaning. "There should be just as much conscience put into dusting a room as in managing an estate," the books said and it was a pronouncement the Victorian housewife took very much to heart. She would begin by draping the furniture in the room with dust covers and opening windows wide to expose all hidden dirt. Cobwebs were dispatched with a cloth-covered broom. Picture frames, mirrors, and curtains were brushed down with a feather duster but a small bellows might be needed to blow the dust from especially ornate carvings on furniture, moldings, frames, etc.

A sprinkling of dampened tea leaves, bran, coffee grounds or even some freshly cut grass kept down the dust as carpets were swept. Only when everything looked "company ready" were the dust covers taken outside, shaken and carried into the next room, where the process would begin again. Windows were often washed weekly. Carpets were sponged clean several times a month. Rugs and draperies were shaken and aired twice a month, even in rooms seldom used. Furthermore, time had to be found for sewing in a world where clothing was still largely made at home, while darning and repairs were an ongoing project picked up automatically when a moment was found to sit.

Even the seasons made their demands. Summer and fall meant canning and preserving, winter brought the holidays, and both spring and fall called for a massive, disruptive housecleaning from top to bottom.

It is no small wonder that housewives took to buying washers and vacuums in mass quantities when American factories supplied chain stores with inexpensive, durable machines. The Boerners made a great deal of money selling these appliances, not to mention finished goods. However, lending truth to the maxim "what goes up must come down," fortunes began deteriorating for the Boerners with the rise of the great American urban department store.

According to Robert W. Wells, author of *Papa Floribunda: A Biography of Eugene S. Boerner*, 1905 marked the beginning of the end of the Boerner clan's dominance over Cedarburg's commercial life. Tragedy first struck when Mrs. Arthur Boerner contracted cancer in that year, lingering on for 20 months. In the meantime, Arthur lost $50,000 he had invested in a northern iron/manganese mine. Drained and saddened by his wife's death, he no longer cared about the mine or his other investments, so the entire business structure the family had built began to crumble from neglect. Teddy Roosevelt made him postmaster in 1906, but the zest for life had seeped out of him. In 1909, he had a stroke, dying weeks later.

A variety of troubles beset the Boerner stores after 1910, including but not limited to competition. The brothers, after Arthur's death in 1909, bought poorly. The interurban line went in, cutting travel time and expense to Schuster's department store in Milwaukee. Many Cedarburgers shopped in the big city for items they had once bought at Boerner Brothers; the brothers responded by extending credit too easily, resulting in heavy losses. To make matters worse, some of the hired clerks were sticky-fingered. Add to that the need to employ evermore family members, and disaster was written on the wall. In 1912 they sold their West Bend store.

By 1914, the business had lost money for several years and stood deep in debt. The Boerners, along with the Armbrusters and other influential families, had invested heavily in a Tolland, Colorado silver mine and general store business. The speculator who sold the Cedarburg families' shares of the mine was a Colorado preacher who turned out to be a crook, and the capital disappeared along with the preacher. To make matters worse, a general business depression hit in 1914 and 1915, and in 1916, Boerner Brothers Manufacturing Association was liquidated. Each of the 13 grandchildren shared an equal share of $468.83, or about $7,000 in 2003 dollars. In 1919, the Port store building was sold to pay off debts, closing in 1928. The Cedarburg store remained open only due to an infusion of capital from a near-relative named Kuether, causing it to be renamed the Boerner-Kuether Store. It, however, closed in 1925. This series of events, according to Wells, spelled the end of the Boerner family's reign "as being regarded in Cedarburg as being among the well-to-do . . ."

This family drama played out against the backdrop of a town in prosperous flux. American culture invaded inexorably, in the form of merchandise, electric lights, minstrel and medicine shows, and traveling carnies. The woolen mill prospered, especially following the 1897 installation of an electric generator used to power the mill and three nearby Wittenberg homes. The factory also heated Diedrich Wittenberg's brick house from across the street by piping in steam from a tunnel that had been blasted from rock below the street. Diedrich also used it to commute to work in the winter and sloppy spring months, saving his spats from a good splattering and his maid some cleaning. In addition to that passage, another tunnel was dug to the dye house across Bridge Street. Both still exist, although they are bricked up now.

Immediately after the new century's dawn, civic leaders in town formed the Cedarburg Advancement Association (CAA). Notes in the Robert Armbruster Archive show that the cream of the second-generation crop attended the CAA's formational meeting in 1902. The list includes Boerners, Schroeders, Brusses, Armbrusters, Wittenbergs, and Hilgens. The CAA acted similar to a chamber of commerce, promoting the city's charms to potential businesses while agitating along with private firms and government agencies to improve the city's infrastructure.

To that end, the CAA actively sought the interurban connection to join themselves to Milwaukee. They chose between two competing plans in a resolution dated March 15, 1905. The interurban went into business in 1906 and travelers could journey from Milwaukee to Sheboygan for 57¢ and in some comfort, not to mention inside of two hours.

The interurban increased traffic to Hilgen Springs Park, paradoxically making it one of the best-known day resorts in Wisconsin while undercutting its more profitable business—resort stays of a week or more. However, with the advent of easy and cheap light rail transportation, the day trade took over, and sometimes as many as 10,000 people would trip up the rail line to picnic in the idylls of Cedar Creek's premier resort. These picnickers pushed out resort-goers, costing Hilgen business. The resort struggled.

Signs that Cedarburg would inevitably be sucked into a sphere of the greater American culture were never so apparent as in the years just before and immediately following the Spanish-American War. At the turn of the century all the town's Lutheran church services were spoken in German, the Catholic in Latin, and only one other denomination even existed. Mono-lingual Lutheran church culture was seen by a handful of influential people (especially merchants such as the Boerners and Kuethers) as holding back assimilation and thereby holding back progress, especially commercial. After failing to convince the Lutheran parishes to give one service a week in English, a group of mostly Immanuel congregants determined to create an English-speaking Lutheran church.

In 1903, they invited Reverend W.K. Frick and Reverend A.C. Anda of the General Council of the Evangelical Lutheran Church to come to Cedarburg from Milwaukee to conduct English services. Since Frick preached the first sermon on the first Sunday in Advent (Ascension Day on May 24, 1904), the

The pea cannery pictured here gave outlet to the many farmers who grew peas in the countryside. Cedarburg was, as too were Ozaukee County and Wisconsin, a major pea producer. (Courtesy of the Robert Armbruster Archive.)

members christened it Evangelical Lutheran Church of the Advent. They changed the name to Advent Lutheran Church, but it was referred to simply as, "Die Englische Kirche," or "The English Church." Reverend Strassburger at Immanuel offered space in their school for services and catechism classes. They met there for months before removing themselves to an empty store a block away.

Charter members of this first English-speaking church in Cedarburg included the families of Fred Wittenberg, George Boerner, Arthur Boerner, Fred Kuether, and Charles Meineke. The Hartungs, Althofens, Fredericksens, Spordlers, Sprivseths, and the Rindts also made up part of that inaugural group.

In 1908, George Boerner presented the church with the land it currently sits upon after the congregation outgrew the storefront. They constructed a stone church and made it ready for its first service on March 13, 1910. The congregation became one of the most active in the city, mirroring the frenetic business activities of its founders. One example was the annual summer picnic at Little Cedar Lake where pictures give evidence that virtually the town's entire leadership gathered for it. Since few automobiles existed, they loaded a horse-drawn hay rack high with children for the trips. The driver allowed the horses to gallop down hill, to the thrill of the children, and to trot over flat roads. However, at the beginning of any ascent, the kids were asked off and told to trudge to the top to meet the plodding and sweating horses.

A few years earlier, in 1900, Reverend H.A. Atkinson, a Methodist pastor in Fredonia and Grafton, found no Protestant English services in Cedarburg. He canvassed the town for interest, and upon finding some, held the first Methodist service in an old saloon in that year. The tiny congregation of 21 souls, just the smallest slip of a Methodist island in a Lutheran and German-speaking lake, had five different pastors giving Methodist sacraments in the first five years.

During this time, a set of women belonging to the congregation organized the Ladies' Aid, which gave financial and material support to the burgeoning church: Mrs. W.H. Wiesler, Mrs. W.H. Rintelmann, Miss Clara Rintelmann, Mrs. J.M. Loomer, Mrs. Charles Tramble, and Mrs George Dunwell. On the fourth anniversary of the Ladies' Aid, they threw a fundraising party described by Tramble in a letter to a friend:

> Each invitation contained a small bag for a penny for each year of the member's age. The gathering was held in a vacant store building near the School building on the opposite side of the street. The store was packed with people that evening and the ladies were perplexed as to how to get the crowd quiet enough to serve lunch. Mr. Danwell assisted the ladies by singing "The Poor Old Slave" so well without any accompaniment that you could hear a pin drop. The lunch was served and the party was a financial success.

The congregation incorporated that year around five trustees: Dr. Wiesler, William Rintelmann, Charles Schumann, E.W. Sweetnam, and Miss Ruth Stow. A new church was planned and built on Portland Avenue, opening in January 1905. As they would for many stone and frame buildings in the coming decades, William Hilgen did the architecture and Vollmar again performed the mason work.

The Cedarburg Police Department had been established in 1885. Between city-hood and the turn of the century many marshals served the community. However, it wasn't until the early 1900s that Otto Beckman became the city's first constable. Beckman was responsible for traffic enforcement in the new automobile age, only he didn't drive a car, didn't know how to, and didn't care to learn. His idea of traffic control was standing on Washington Avenue at the base of the hill on the north side of town and using a stop watch to clock speeders between two posts. If he blew his whistle at an offender, they were expected to stop for him and be ticketed. However, because he had no car to pursue those who did not stop, any scofflaws escaped scot-free. Occasionally, if called upon to visit a farm or neighboring town, the city provided a rental car complete with driver. The city's leaders, wanting to ensure that Otto was indeed on foot patrol, installed time clocks at Fireman's Park on the north end and the Canning Company on the south side to be punched twice a night during his tour of duty.

The turn of the century was a curious time, one still redolent with traditions hundreds of years old but carrying the sheen and polish of the new and the manufactured. Following the custom of Middle Age Germany, the bells of the

The original Cedarburg Volunteer Fire Station is pictured here—a beautifully constructed cream city brick structure. The brick work shows a high degree of sophistication, especially in the arches over the doors and along the cornices and other trim. (From the Rappold Collection.)

churches in Cedarburg rang every Saturday night. In the Old World they chimed to frighten away evil spirits before services the next day. Yet in twentieth-century Cedarburg, it was taken as a signal to warm bath water on the great rectangular cook-stoves and fill wooden tubs placed in the kitchen, so that, in strict order of precedence beginning "mit Vater," the family would take their weekly baths.

Following the tradition begun in the Vaterland, the church bell was also rung when a congregation member died, once for every year of life, three separate times. This tradition continued through the first half of the century in Cedarburg, giving generations of people all over town pause as they put down the task at hand and counted together as a community, speculating on which of their neighbors had died. However, these tolls didn't always paint the final stroke on the canvass of life. One modern-thinking Cedarburg woman had kept her birth date a secret in life, causing considerable confusion around town as the bells gave up her mystery in the afterlife.

One European tradition the older Teutons who created the bund by the creek did not miss was war. As noted earlier, civic leaders of Cedarburg expressed little enthusiasm for the last American war. This new generation, however, grew up untried by hardship and utterly inexperienced with war's travails and grief. When the nation's Yellow Press began agitating for military intervention against Spain and its possessions in 1898, Cedarburg's youths responded to the call to arms enthusiastically. Fifteen boys from the town and surrounding area formed a company named Dewey Guards after the famous Admiral Thomas Dewey. Their leader and drill master was a Milwaukeean, Captain Reade.

Women in town formed a Relief Corps, later joining the Milwaukee chapter to coordinate efforts. The Relief Corps canvassed the town for donations and received enough subscriptions to buy a flag and send-off packets of buttons, thread, combs, and other personal items for each man. The Cedarburg Woolen Mill gave each Dewey Guard a woolen blanket as well.

The company drilled every evening in the village square between the Washington House and the mill, and immediately joined Company E out of Milwaukee when the call came. They departed for Camp Douglas on the Fourth of July after a banquet was held in their honor at the Washington House. John Grundtke, one of the town's Civil War veterans, gave a nostalgic send-off address. The Guard then marched as a unit to the railroad depot, followed by a crowd and accompanied by the town band.

In September, after training, the army transferred them to Camp Anniston in Alabama, where they spent the winter months. By spring, the war ended and they were released from duty, never having left American soil. Upon their return, the Guards donated their flag to the Cedarburg Women's Club.

An odd incident occurred around this time, one displaying the cracks that had formed around the foundation of the Teutonic Utopia. The justice of the peace in 1904 was John Armbruster, who kept impeccable records of his activities. Those records contain a tale of a tragic mystery still unsolved.

On March 3, 1904, farmer Hermann Zeunert told Armbruster that a dog had dragged a dead baby to his house, so he stored the body in the outhouse until Armbruster and the physician, Alfred Kreutzer, could arrive to investigate.

The Dewey Guards sport their new wool blankets, gifts from the Cedarburg Woolen Mill. They would come in handy as the Guard wintered in Alabama before returning home not having seen any action, let alone any Spanish-speakers. (From the Rappold Collection.)

Within hours, calls for a jury to convene an inquest were answered with the arrivals of F.R. Kuether, John Lauterbach, and four others. In the presence of the baby and around the table in Kuether's room, the jury was sworn in. They decided instantly to call the district attorney by phone, who assured the men he would be in Cedarburg the following day. Subpoenas were issued to Zeunert, Mrs. August Groth, Mrs. Frank Reynolds, Mrs. Bertha Sohrweide, Miss Lena Brandt, Dr. Kreutzer, and Miss Bertha Koepsel, and all appeared at the inquest. The district attorney requested the inquiry be a closed session and all non-participants were asked to leave. What took place behind those closed doors is anyone's guess, as there are no records to document the truth of the matter. However, no charges were brought and neither the identity of the baby or its mother were ever revealed to the public.

Regarding the fire department, the turn of the century seemed both stable and tumultuous. E.G. Wurthman was elected chief in 1889 and served 23 years, overseeing several station moves and the city's worst fire disaster—the burning of the firehouse itself. Having moved the station from behind Turner Hall to one location near downtown, and finally to the old schoolhouse on Washington Avenue (this last by state mandate in 1894), the chief anticipated decades of use from their new firehouse. Yet it operated from the location for only 14 years before it burned to the ground in 1907.

At 2 a.m. on a Tuesday morning immediately after Easter a passerby spotted the flames. He put up a call, but even before the townsfolk could come out and contribute any help, the whole interior of the brick building was aflame. Soon, high winds blew flames and cinders over to the adjoining Cedarburg House, owned by Mrs. Kuether and one of the oldest in the city, involving it as well. Flames spread to a barn at the rear of the home, completely consuming it. Friends and neighbors rushed in the fire-lit night to vacate the household goods before they met a fiery end.

The Grafton Fire Department arrived within minutes, Thiensville's not much later, to do battle with the fire after being advised by telegraph. Cedarburg also asked Milwaukee for assistance; they had just placed an engine on a flatbed train car when they were notified that the fire was finally under control. A Mr. Maas of the Thiensville lumber yard got word of the fire, hitched his team, and raced over to help, but upon his arrival his horses dropped dead from exhaustion.

The fire, while devastating the community and leaving it bereft of fire protection for some time, also provided an opportunity. The state had recently mandated that the city build a high school and since the grade school was only yards away from the now-vacant lot, it seemed to be the logical site to build upon. The cornerstone of the Washington Building, now the site of City Hall, was laid May 3, 1908. The city erected it with rock-faced Anschutz Limestone, just as they had next door at the Lincoln Building, at a cost of $30,000.

The city also built a new cream brick fire station and jail house (with city offices above) on Mequon street. CFD hired Samuel Kannenberg, a local wagon maker, to build a hose wagon and a hook and ladder that were horse drawn (which CFD still has, bringing out for the annual Fourth of July parade). The hand-picked team chosen to pull the new wagons were called the "Wild Ones" because of their spirited nature. In one instance after answering a call, they shied and galloped off, crashing into a front porch on a Washington Avenue home.

Ernst Schneider, born in 1877 in Milwaukee, took over from Wurthman as chief in 1915 and served until his death in the late 1950s. Many credit Schroeder with developing the department's reputation for quality and professionalism, as well as building it into the community service organization it is known for. Under Schneider, the CFD made its first purchase of motorized equipment in 1926, a Dodge Chemical Truck. Two years later they bought a Pirsch 600-gallon truck as well as a hook and ladder. The town of Cedarburg contracted the CFD in 1936 for ten years, so they expanded by adding an 800-gallon truck to haul water out to the farms under their jurisdiction. The CFD also became a member of the Wisconsin State Firemen's Association (WSFA) in the early 1920s, bringing home many awards from the annual tournaments held at the convention. In 1925, Adlai Horn and the Cedarburg American Legion Band went to the Watertown WSFA Convention and bid for the convention to be hosted by Cedarburg the following year. Their creative effort resulted in the convention's arrival two years later—on the 60th birthday of the CFD.

Other signs of civic assimilation into the American system sprang up, especially in the area of city infrastructure. No more would the European system do for these Americans; they would have all the modern conveniences. To light homes and businesses, the city created the Cedarburg Light and Water Commission. The 1906 act gave the mayor power to construct the needed plant, wires, poles, etc., which provided Cedarburg with heat, light, and power through electricity. The commission approached their purely American task with Teutonic gravity and stability, establishing enough profit to pay for constant improvements to the power grid for years.

Another incursion by the American system, indoor plumbing, arrived in the early 1920s with a vengeance. Until then everyone in the burg used outdoor plumbing, with creek-side dwellers using outhouses extending over the creek. The city installed a sewer system in 1921 and 1922 and then passed an ordinance that gave *all* households in the city just one year to install indoor plumbing.

The city also installed a new gravity water system at the same time as the sewage system. Before then, residents obtained water through wells or directly out of the creek. However, in late fall and early spring, these wells constituted a public health hazard, since the ground water levels were too "high" or the ground was too cold to act as a "filter bed" to water-borne diseases like cholera and diphtheria. The water towers, filtration system, and efficient sewage removal solved the public health problem.

It seemed that, with a new high school, fire station, and church, the town was building in stone as though its supply would soon run dry. But the stone was everywhere and easy to quarry, so other brick and stone buildings cropped up in the years following the century's turn.

Unfortunately, when fire struck the fire station the city was left with no way to battle the blaze and the structure burnt to the ground, as seen in this picture. Another fire station and city hall replaced it and the site was used for a high school. (From the Rappold Collection.)

The bank was built in 1908 with a Romanesque facade and the same distinctive Cedarburg heavy rock face limestone blocks and thick mortar used in the schools. It would later hold the telephone exchange on the second floor. Armbruster's built their current store, a distinctive and elegantly white-glazed terra-cotta-faced structure, in 1908. Brown Street Clock Co. of Monessen, Pennsylvania made the now-rare cast iron sidewalk clock for the Armbrusters. So many buildings in the small town by that point were stone or brick that Cedarburg inherited the moniker "the City with a Face of Stone" from neighboring communities.

The entire city and countryside prospered in the boom years before World War I. The population remained steady, but businesses and merchants seemed to thrive. By 1904, the pea cannery operated by the ever-enterprising Wittenbergs was up and running, as was a foundry by Gus Zunker and a soda maker, J. Winger and Brothers, which would later become Geo. Ritter's Beverages. Herman Zuenert bought the Burger and Crittenden Elevator Company next to the depot, and delivered baskets of coal by horse-drawn truck to households for heat, even as farmers traveled past him to deliver loads of malt barley to his elevators. These crops of barley and hops would be weighed, loaded, and shipped to Milwaukee's thriving beer plants.

But storm clouds gathered on the horizon as war rumblings from the European continent made way to Cedarburg, causing deep anxiety. In fact, most of the Teutons in Cedarburg had mixed feelings about the war after it broke out in 1914.

This photo shows both the new Fire House and City Hall and the power generation station. These structures sit on the east side of the creek due north and across the street from the mill. (From the Wirth Family Archive.)

They had concerns about the ability of their German relatives to withstand the hardships of war. Cedarburg residents transferred funds to Europe through the Turn Verein, Lutheran churches, and other agencies, but recalling the tyrannical nature of past Teutonic governments, they made sure to send their financial support directly to families, not the German government. An anti-German government attitude already reigned in the Cedarburg Bund when America entered the war, and many thought that the United States had been given just cause to enter the war when the *Lusitania* was sunk in 1917. The upright Teutons of Cedarburg could not tolerate submarine warfare and loss of innocent lives, and while no one wanted war against their German relatives, they viewed going to battle against German rulers as justifiable.

Adlai Horn wrote later that feelings about World War I in Cedarburg were indeed mixed because of the nuances the issue raised. While many would gladly send their sons to fight on behalf of the federal government when facing tyranny, many had relatives in Germany and did not favor going to war against family. Still perhaps cognizant of the violence that afflicted others of German heritage who spoke out against the war in places like Milwaukee and St. Louis, Cedarburgers voiced no opposition to war. However, one indication that unspoken anti-war opinion ran high came up in the 1918 election when Victor Berger, the German Milwaukee Socialist outspoken in his opposition to the war, ran for the state senate. He swept Cedarburg in the voting, gaining nearly 90 percent of the vote.

A Milwaukee passenger on the interurban precipitated ill will against Cedarburg when he witnessed a town parade where a German group (probably the Turners) carried a German-like flag. Word got to the Milwaukee press that Cedarburg was a hotbed of anti-American, pro-German sentiment. The *Milwaukee Journal*, on May 27, 1918, predicted the end of "Deutschtum," or Germanism, in a diatribe:

> Here, in this trusting, peace-loving land of ours, Deutschtum has in truth been a hydra-headed monster. Evil, cunning, sinuous, it has worked and plotted in our schools, using its language to inculcate moral treason in the unsuspecting minds of children; it has used the church, the Temples of God, to serve its wicked purposes . . .

While these charges against Cedarburg weren't entirely true, many in town were irritated when others took extreme actions like book burning, renaming sauerkraut and German fried potatoes to Liberty Cabbage and French Fries, not to mention issuing anti-German diatribes. Whipping up war fever and the propaganda that characterized Germans as "Huns" and "Krauts" devastated the Teutonic people of Cedarburg. Parishioners made calls for English-speaking services at the still German-only Lutheran churches, and organizations such as the Turn Verein began keeping their minutes in English. Some families Anglicized their names and stopped attending German cultural activities like the Liederkranz and German-language plays (long popular in Turner Hall). What assimilation couldn't accomplish through commerce and technology, the war completed. Cedarburg, still over 90 percent German, now tried to become as much like the rest of America as quickly as possible.

Regardless of the propaganda and its effects on the town's culture, Cedarburg sent a good deal of money and many of its men to fight on behalf of the British and French in Europe. Eugene Boerner, grandson of Frederick, volunteered for the army in October 1917, joining the Air arm. He learned to fly in Dallas, writing home later, "Flying is great." To another friend he said, "To hell with your old Ford, I'd sooner hit a convection current up high, going over a woods, a road, or a pond. . . .I think of old Henry floating along on one wheel and I let her ride the waves." He never did fly in battle, as the war ended immediately after he graduated flight school.

According to *Wisconsin in the World War* by R.B. Pixley, George Ayers was the first Cedarburger to die in the war, on July 18, 1918. Peter Wollner, a Cedarburg resident who died as a result of an accident on October 15, 1918, had the American Legion Post named in his honor. Palmer Wirth also served and survived, and in a letter home dated May 17, 1918, he wrote of his discovery that the rest of the people in the country weren't quite like those he knew in Cedarburg:

> Most of the fellows here haven't had a fair chance in life. One fellow's dad was a heavy booze fighter, his mother dead and family broke up. Had to leave home at age of 11 yrs and took up fishing and later got on

Despite anti-German feeling and propaganda, many Cedarburg youths served valiantly in the First World War. This picture shows the returning warriors on the steps of Turner Hall in 1919. (From the Rappold Collection.)

board here. I used to hate these lads because they looked so tough but sort of pity them because they all have a tough luck story to tell.

Another letter from Wirth dated 1919 and from London detailed how impressed he was with the architecture (and girls) of London.

F.W. Boerner wrote home saying that people in France had a different lifestyle than Americans. In a letter from France dated April 21, 1918, he wrote:

All the people live in towns. Very seldom do we see a farmhouse standing alone. The towns are only a few miles apart at the most. Everything is stone and red tiles roofing. Have not seen a frame house since we're in France. We sleep in a hay mow, but we are getting along fine and everything is O.K.

Liberty Loans, bonds sold to fund the war effort, went on sale in Ozaukee County in 1918; the first subscription raised $67,500. There was a second, third, fourth, and even a fifth bond issue and subscription. The total raised in the county topped an astounding $2 million.

120

World War I helped the woolen mill, but depression followed and sales fell off considerably. At virtually the same time as the war's end, another blow befell the Germans in Cedarburg—Prohibition. For decades, the "drys" had tried to regulate and even outlaw alcohol. The anti-German sentiment generated by the war benefitted the cause of prohibitionists once they connected beer and the Kaiser, dubbing the beverage "Kaiser brew." Historians note that the passage of the Volstead Act in 1919 effectively stripped the German-American people of their main form of socialization.

This wasn't the only ill wind blowing. A nativist Congress bowed to pressure from Yankees who felt threatened by recent immigration and thus passed 1924's Johnson Reed Act, designed to restrict immigration from southern and eastern Europe while reflecting the following attitude: "Moreover, Americanization should occur voluntarily and willingly on the part of the foreign population. Any national group that remained isolate, or distinct, constituted a potential threat to American life and, as such, must be viewed with suspicion." The flood of refugees and immigrants from Europe slowed to a trickle. And so much for Teutonic Utopias.

The economic depression after the war matched the newfound depression of Cedarburg's residents; a nagging doubt had crept into their proud Teutonic souls. This despondency manifested itself in many ways, but most profoundly in the once-enterprising community's inability to create new industry or to generate traction in a sputtering national economy. The Cedarburg Advancement Association, beset by the loss of influential leaders and multiple hits from war

These Liberty Loan promoters pause in front of the power station; you can see the mill behind them. Cedarburg contributed more than most small communities to the Liberty Loan effort, in addition to having sent many dollars to German family and friends. (From the Rappold Collection.)

and Prohibition, stopped meeting completely in 1918 until the middle of the next decade, and then only intermittently. The Turn Verein withered away and became a shell of its former self in the post-war era, running on sheer inertia and little else. Few people in the community felt courageous enough at this point to trumpet their involvement in a German club, even if it was a benevolent society.

By the late 1920s, Cedarburg found itself unprepared for the new national economy, treading in a backwater market without an adequate water transportation route, stagnating with no nearby natural resources or raw materials to make manufacturing cheap, and functioning without a sufficiently cheap power supply. The town had reached a plateau concerning growth and, it seemed, on leadership and vision. Civic leaders, while pushing the town into the twentieth century by building roads, sewers, and throwing up power lines, offered no ingenious ideas about how the town could capitalize on its Teutonic heritage and population, or on the environment around them. The wind went out of the city's sails and captains of Cedarburg industry, despite their blandishments and well-intentioned efforts, could not bluster the riggings full as Father Hilgen and Company had once done.

By 1929, the mill was losing money and was shut down. It reopened later in the year to produce new textiles such as orlon, rayon, and nylon, but competition from much larger, more modern and efficient mills caused it to close in 1968. The dearth of industry and new enterprise made Cedarburg, a once vital manufacturing and milling community, almost totally dependent on agriculture. The Teutonic utopia that had once benefited from a completely diversified economy now relied primarily on its dairies and creameries, and to a lesser extent on its pea farmers and cannery, its home-style meats and sausages, and sweet-corn production. By decade's end, 1 in 20 acres of Ozaukee County land was expressly devoted to peas, helping the state become the largest producer and canner of peas in the world.

No influx of immigrants waited in the wings to rescue Cedarburg either. The Boerner family was moribund and the Hilgens all but disappeared, having closed the Hilgen Manufacturing plant some years earlier and operating Hilgen Spring Park in Prohibition time as an amusement park (an attempt doomed from the start). The wilderness had been tamed and a Teutonic utopia built, but now, in this American Century, it seemed all for naught. The farmers and merchants of Cedarburg struggled forward with no visionary to guide them, stumbling through a newfound wilderness of bramble and briar, an economic wasteland without even a beer to quench their collective German thirst.

That is until Elmer Kiekhaefer and Stephen Fischer came along.

122

9. Depression, War, Boom

World War was quelled. Fascism and Nazism and Imperialism had all been crushed under the weight of American Industrialism by men and women who wished nothing more than to live in freedom and peace. Nine million came home, and $23 billion in war contracts were cancelled. Fearing depression, the American Congress provided GI loans that would house them all and, eventually, create today's consumer society. Roads were built out to vast stretches of former farmland and wilderness that suddenly contained homes and schools needing filling. Student loans were guaranteed creating a populace with a level of education never before seen on this planet. America was moving, alright, into the future and at federal highway speeds.

    –Rick Magnussen, in a thesis entitled "World War Two Started All This"

The Roaring Twenties, that time of speculation in stocks and land, never really touched rural and relatively isolated Cedarburg. The merchants had invested their earnings in the town, just as the industrialists had. Farmers with any extra cash built cooperative dairies and invested in the pea cannery, or perhaps the shoe factory. And so most of the cash generated in Cedarburg stayed in Cedarburg; the Teutons invested in confidence, and they find that in their neighbors, not in land speculators in Florida or in heavy machinery manufacturers in nearby Milwaukee.

This "investment entrenchment" affected the town in a couple of different ways. First, it kept Cedarburg from riding the bubble of faux prosperity that enveloped much of the nation. While business was good in the 1920s, it was not great in Cedarburg. The population did grow for the first time since before the century's turn, but only about 15 percent, and that is after 30 years of no real growth. A cycle of trade existed in which merchants sold to the farmers, who sold to the dairies and canners, who sold to the urban masses, who made the goods that Cedarburg merchants then sold to the farmers. The small industries in Cedarburg employed a handful of residents and sold their goods regionally, but because the town lacked natural resources, power, and special expertise, everything remained small. The time of great mills and a purely nineteenth-century regional economy had passed and Cedarburg was, in the 1920s, just another farm town in a vast nation of agriculture communities.

Ginseng was king, at least king of the cash crops in the area around Cedarburg. Here one gets an idea of how labor intensive the harvesting of the roots was. (From the Rappold Collection.)

The second effect of the "investment entrenchment" was insulation from the worst of the Depression. In the very late 1920s, when the speculative bubble burst and investors across the nation were seeking tall buildings from which to leap, Cedarburgers avoided the largest losses since they did business primarily among themselves, with few large customers in the "ausland." Their money was not "out there" in stocks or land, but in the town itself.

A couple of products grown or raised in Cedarburg that had national or international import did exist. The first was ginseng, a root with highly regarded medicinal value in China. According to Cedarburg resident John Malone's 1930 book called *The Ginseng Growers' Guide*, prices in 1930 were between $5 for the lowest grade and $13 for the highest—*per pound*—with wild ginseng bringing a $5 bonus per pound on top of that. This was the market when farmers were receiving just $1 for a *bushel* of corn. Cultivating 1 acre of ginseng could yield 4,000 pounds of dry roots, or between $20,000 and $52,000 per acre. Since the dollar was worth about a tenth of what it is in 2003, adding a zero to the figures makes it is easy to see the high stakes involved with this cash crop.

A pamphlet issued by the Chinese government named "The Present Ginseng Market in China" demonstrates the demand:

> Cultivated Ginseng: . . . attractive in shape and of golden color, well wrinkled and breaks snow-white, etc. If you have this kind of root, we shall pay you wild root prices [higher due to speculation] . . . If your lot is large enough we will send our buyer specially to see you.

Ginseng grows well in wooded areas and only once on any given spot, so the available land for cultivation was fast disappearing in China, but the woods of Cedarburg were ideal for this root, as the Malones and the Fromm family found. Malone wrote, "Ginseng plants have been found to grow the best in localities where hardwood timber has once grown." They don't need tending in the summer, either, after planting and shading. "One man can look after three acres in the summer," said Malone. Gathering and storing ginseng in the fall and winter and drying the roots thereafter is labor intensive, so ginseng farms provided a reliable and important source of employment in Cedarburg through the 1920s and 1930s.

Fox farming shined as another bright economic light in and around Cedarburg. As comprehensively examined in *Bright With Silver*, a book by Katherine Pinkerton, the Fromm family came to the Mequon area in the early 1920s to grow ginseng and raise foxes. Since farming the animals is expensive to capitalize, the Fromms used ginseng on their farms to raise the needed funds. Four brothers coordinated efforts to develop this enterprise across the world: Walter took care of ginseng, Edward handled business matters and was the source of ideas, Henry cared for the foxes, and John bred them to have a distinctive silver tip to their fur, something never before done. Once success was achieved with this pattern, they took the world fox market by storm and the family became the largest fur supplier in the entire world.

The Cedarburg connection grew out of marriage when their sister Erna Fromm married a cousin, Edwin Nieman, son of banker and pea cannery owner John F.

Fox farms spread out over the Cedarburg farmland, taking hundreds of acres from crops and devoting them to fox. Tens of thousands of these fox huts would spring up, and the result would be tens of millions of dollars pumped into the local economy while the rest of the nation suffered from the Depression. (From the Rappold Collection.)

Nieman, in 1920. Nieman saw the potential for profit in furs and joined the brothers to form the Fromm Brothers-Nieman Company in 1920, with a main ranch located in Thiensville. They bought land at a frantic pace, soon reaching into the Town of Cedarburg, building fox houses just a stone's throw outside the city itself.

They employed, in 1922, at least a dozen permanent hands on the farm to grow ginseng, handle the milk herd, and care for foxes. By that year ginseng brought in $45,000 to $115,000 annually—an astonishing sum for a small farm, but they needed every dime to finance the fox investment, which hadn't yet turned a profit. Soon though, their silver-tipped fox business had reached the black. In 1923, the Fromms' fur sales came to $35,000, increasing to almost a quarter of a million dollars in 1924, and in 1925 nearly half a million. In 1926, they received a check from market for $785,000 and crossed the million-dollar threshold the following year, becoming known as the finest foxers in America. The Nieman family wanted more say in running the business in 1928 when they took in $1.33 million, so in 1929, the two families split the business with Nieman taking the northernmost (nearest Cedarburg) farms.

While the Depression forced them to market more aggressively, they stayed successful by creating a line of sewn fur clothing and coats. The move started a national trend toward multiple fox pelt cloaks and wraps. Even at Depression prices, the beauty added enough value and sales volume to see the Fromms and Niemanns through those depression years in which many businesses died on the vine.

These bright spots in the local economy, as well as the penchant for investing within the community by Cedarburgers, made the Depression easier to to swallow, as many recall. There were no soup lines, as in the major cities. There wasn't an exodus to any other state, as happened throughout the Plains region. There were no mass business failures, as witnessed in areas reliant on manufacturing and exports. Farms and gardens in the area brought forth bounteous plenty and the populace ate fairly well, even if it was off old china while wearing patched and threadbare clothing.

Most longtime businesses in Cedarburg did show effects of the slow-down, such as the Boerner's landscaping business run by Art, Eugene, and a couple of other brothers that fell on hard times beginning in 1932. This forced most of them to find other ways to make ends meet. Art once received a letter from wife Gladys while traveling his route selling tractors, in which she weighed in on the Depression's effects: "Had some kraut and neck bones today—the latter were 3 pounds for 10 cents. 14 cents gives us meat for two days. Tomorrow at least half will get browned with spuds. So near to back bones brings back childhood days."

Even through trying times, the preoccupation with growing things stuck with two of the Boerner progeny, although they needed to leave the confines of Cedarburg to prosper. Eugene, grandson of C. Frederick and son of Arthur, left Cedarburg after the war and became an internationally known rose hybridizer. This started in an Arkansas nursery and then blossomed at a Newark, New Jersey nursery, called Jackson & Perkins, where he gained honors for improving the

Floribunda rose. In 1949, the Fashion rose, invented by Eugene, became the first rose to win nine international prizes.

His brother Arthur went on to become a landscape architect and manager of Milwaukee's County Park System after developing the system with Charles B. Whitnall. He created a botanical garden that carries his name, along with his brother's roses in what is regarded as one of the finest arboretums in the world (over a million visitors a year).

At the same time, Cedarburg and its people went about the ritual of "business as usual." Tony Fischer, brother of the man who would soon become mayor, explains his experience working ten hour days as a child through the Depression at the woolen mill:

> I was employed as a duster in the woolen mill as my first job in the depression. I shook dust out of the wool as it come [*sic*] from the dryer. The wool was washed and then dried at 120 degrees. I had to hang a towel from the ceiling to use for drying my eyes it was so wet. I felt like I just come out of the creek. I also mixed the wool in the dye vat; I was so small I had to hang off the end of the eight foot pole I used.

When peas came in from the fields, the cannery went on overtime, employing everyone not already working elsewhere, with many dropping their own jobs to help out. Bob Armbruster still has pay receipts showing 16 hour days and an 81 hour work week—for which he was paid $60.03.

The Woolen Mill was still a major source of jobs, along with the pea cannery and the ginseng and fox farms. However much there was to eat because of the surrounding farmland, through the Depression most people in Cedarburg had to scrabble to make ends meet, although the worst was experienced elsewhere in the nation. (From the Rappold Collection.)

The Excelsior Shoe and Slipper Company exemplified the endogamous business practices of the town. Every merchant or businessman owned at least a small piece of Excelsior, and no one from out of town did. Likewise, few businessmen owned stock in companies not located in Cedarburg. This practice had two effects: before the Depression it kept a lid on growth, and during the Depression it protected Cedarburgers from the worst of the losses. (Courtesy of the Robert Armbruster Archive.)

Perhaps the most telling set of exchanges comes in the form of a series of letters sent to a Cedarburg mother by her ex-patriot son in New Jersey. Werner (Mel) Meyer's father Fred taught at Immanuel school for 33 years, marrying Othilie Pollock before moving to Cedarburg in 1895, where he and Reverend Strassburger conducted classes together. Mel's father (note the anglicizing of his German name, Werner) became known to all within the community as "Teacher Meyer." The paraphrased and excerpted letters below were all mailed to Othilie from Mel's home in New Jersey. They tell a tale of how rapidly conditions of the depression changed and brought about struggle, hardship, and strain to family relationships.

December 3, 1931: Mel's brother, still living in Cedarburg, refinanced the house for Othilie. Mel informed her that payment on the note was now just $55 a month, promising to take care of half the monthly dues. "I have been so busy for the last month that I am not afraid of losing my job just yet." He also offered to contribute money for coal, but his brother told him she had enough for heat, so he bought a coat for her instead and sent $10 towards that Christmas gift.

December 9: His bank closed. "This bank closing has strapped us tight as I never thought or hoped to be again. Last week they decided it would remain indefinitely closed . . . we'd be lucky if we eventually got 25 percent of what we have in it."

December 12: He continues, "Received my biggest Christmas present yesterday—bigger even than the bank failure—when Mr. Fry announced a general pay cut of 10% . . . now the future looks rather glum. It will be five or six years before I ever make as much again as I did make. Agatha [his wife] and I sat down and pared our budgets to the bone—everything except plenty of milk for the youngsters and good food for ourselves." He tried to convince his mother to make up papers for a second mortgage to protect his and his brother's investment in her Cedarburg house since his share totaled $2,205. Evidently she already had a second, so he asked instead for receipts to demonstrate that he'd given her money.

January 5, 1932: "The Bakers [friends of theirs in New Jersey] are going to let their house go back to the bank. Jennis' are talking about it, and will do so if Lou gets another pay cut. A large number of homes in our section are being sold for taxes and at mortgage foreclosures."

January 6: He reluctantly revised his mother's share of the mortgage note down from $2,205 to $1,386.90 after being reminded by his mother that she'd paid some of his school expenses in the 1920s.

The CAA aggressively sought to recruit business, even building spaces for factories. A note in the Armbruster archive shows a collection taken from the CAA for $3,000, at $500 per contributor, in an attempt to build a factory to convince the Reinhard Mitten Corporation to relocate. The CAA also promoted the town as "The City of Homeowners" everywhere possible in hopes of gaining industry. In a letter from the *Milwaukee Sentinel*, the advertising manager congratulates Cedarburg for "being the first to take advantage of the growing tendency to 'get away from the city.' "

Still, business growth was nonexistent and even fell back. Taxable property valuations for the county fell five percent between 1930 and 1940 (from $39 million to $37 million) even as the city's population grew from just over 2,000 to 2,245. Hilgen Spring Park struggled, recasting itself as an amusement park complete with rides and a carnival. Other businesses moved into and out of Cedarburg, including General Wood Products and Jayef Hosiery. Some old enterprises

Bands and music were integral parts of Cedarburg life. This photo shows the Mandolin and Guitar Orchestra, one of the seemingly countless bands that practiced and performed at the drop of a hat. (From the Wirth Family Archives.)

simply closed their doors, such as Hanson Canning Machinery (1923–1939) and the Cedarburg Theater (once named the Chimes Theater when it opened in the 1910s, which closed soon after the Rivoli Theater opened in Boerner's old store), yet places like Fromm's fox farms thrived despite conditions and employed many with seasonal work. Although it wasn't easy, if people worked several jobs and watched their expenses, they could survive.

The Depression, for all its detrimental effects on citizens and businesses in Cedarburg, had the positive effect of funneling federal monies into the town. Works Progress Administration money funded a new school gymnasium, city park, sewage treatment plant, the rebuilding of the Columbia bridge, and a swimming pool on the creek above the woolen mills. Federal dollars also financed tuberculosis clinics when the disease ran rampant.

It was a tough period, especially when scarlet fever broke out in 1935, but merchants were able to hold their own. Sandy Wirth recalls that his family's store became, in the 1930s and 1940s, the largest retailer in the county by first selling farm implements and later adding household appliances, shoes, and clothing. "We sold a lot of gas motor-driven washers and driers to the farmers who didn't have electricity yet."

Music and bands were an integral part of Cedarburg life, especially in the 1930s when everyone was looking for a release from the negativity all around them. The city boasted two bands, one civic and the other a fire department band. Ed Rappold claims that Cedarburgers would parade for any reason at all; there are so few people on sidewalks in older photos of parades because almost everyone in town was marching. In 1934, the Peter Wollner Post donated money to build a bandstand in the newly constructed park, which survives to this day. In 1941, band parents organized a high school band, which practiced above the new gymnasium and was popular in parades and exhibitions around the state.

During this time, a man was growing to maturity on a nearby farm who would pick Cedarburg up by the lapels and shake it back into industrial life. As Jeff

Elmer "Carl" Kiekhaefer shows off his new Gull Wing Mercedes sports car in front of Armbruster's Jewelers. Kiekhaefer was enamored of any engine and especially of any fast engine. He would sponsor many NASCAR champions and numerous speedboat champs. (Courtesy of the Robert Armbruster Archive.)

This aerial view of downtown Cedarburg shows how important Kiekhaefer's plant was to the city. It sits just behind and to the left of the Lincoln Building, a short one block walk away. The plant eventually employed hundreds. (Photo by Harold Dobberpuhl.)

Rodengen relates in his book *Iron Fist: The Lives of Carl Kiekhaefer*, Cedarburg would never be the same after Kiekhaefer was born in 1906 as Elmer Heinrich Carl Kiekhaefer. Kiekhaefer so hated the sound of his Christian name that he cut off the German-sounding parts when he became an adult, shortening it to Carl Kiekhaefer. He took the world's smallest marine propulsion company and made it the largest within 20 years, and was granted over 200 patents before he died in 1983. His genius for machinery, and especially small engines, made him a national force in automobile (NASCAR) and speedboat racing. His plant in Cedarburg would, at its height, employ hundreds of people and manufacture tens of millions of dollars in outboard motors.

The Kiekhaefer roots run deep in Cedarburg. Great-grandfather Carl and great-grandmother Friedericka came to Cedarburg in 1850, settling between Mequon and Cedarburg on Port Washington Road. They owned heavily forested land, harvesting logs and sending them to Milwaukee via a small dock constructed on Lake Michigan. Heinrich, Carl's grandfather, took over the family farm in 1876 and created a dairy farm. Arnold, Carl's father, and Clara (nee Wessel) greeted the birth of their son Elmer with great joy and expectation, as he would be the son the couple would rely upon to work the family farm in their retirement. The entire family lived under the unspoken, unwritten code of the frontier—an uncompromising, inflexible, and absolute work ethic—and applied it to farming.

131

Carl, however, had a special affinity for tools and mechanical devices, working on anything involving moving parts. His father bought the first mechanical tractor in Cedarburg, a machine that fascinated Carl. People who knew him then recall that he was always working in the barn, clanking and banging when the harvest was the most important issue at hand. Ed Rappold, whose uncle lived across the road and who would help the Kiekhaefers as good neighbors would do for one another, said "Whenever I helped my uncle, Carl was always working on those machines of his while we got in the harvest." Father and son butted heads over his mechanical interests and he finally left after a blowup in 1925 to take an engineering job in Milwaukee before taking a position for Magnetic Manufacturing, a firm specializing in small motors. By 1938, he had become chief engineer of the company.

Carl's uncle, John Blank, was mayor of Cedarburg, head of Cedarburg Mutual Fire Insurance Company, and generally considered to be the leading booster of town at the time. Blank had lured Thor Hansen to town in 1934 from A.O. Smith to create a small motor factory on a failed site, the Cedarburg Manufacturing Company. Yet by 1938, the business was hemorrhaging money and failing. The Cedarburg State Bank, whose vice president at the time was Edgar Roth, decided they could no longer risk lending the firm money and made plans to buy out Hansen and have someone else take it over. Blank went to Kiekhaefer to enlist him in their scheme, so along with Palmer Wirth, Adlai Horn, Roth, Dr. Wiesler, and Matthew Becker he raised $25,000 in capital to buy out the Cedarburg Manufacturing Company to create Kiekhaefer's new plant. Carl took possession on January 22, 1939, naming it Kiekhaefer Corporation. He jumped out of the gate with his Mercury outboard motor, and it became a huge seller in 1940 by supplying two major chains of stores with 32,000 outboards that year, second only to Evinrude Outboards in national sales.

While in New York at a sales show in January 1940, just a year after taking the factory over, Carl received a tip from somebody in the plant that the bank was trying to sell him out. Edgar Roth had received an offer for the firm from Flambeau, a competitor, for 50 percent more than the original investment. The board of directors worked incessantly to accept the offer while keeping it behind Carl's back. He raced home from New York to find that the bank and investors had decided that "you can never take a loss taking a profit," and were determined to sell the factory from under his feet.

Carl fought hard against the sale, pointing out that he had made $300,000 in sales in his first year, and would likely double it in the next. He made headway one investor at a time. He finally won the day, persuading enough of the board to reject the bid and wait for even higher returns, but he would never forget nor forgive. He took into consideration Cedarburg's civic leaders eagerness to take short-term gains at the expense of long-term profits and found retribution when he chose Fond Du Lac over Cedarburg for a later expansion.

Already in 1940, Kiekhaefer Mercury Marine was the city's largest employer, with more than 100 employees, and "Carl's reputation for no-nonsense business was beginning to spread like the growing smoke from his engine test cells." The onset of war would expand the business exponentially, fueling Cedarburg's tremendous growth through and immediately after World War II.

Meanwhile, a local institution was replacing the mostly defunct Turners as the town's benevolent society and social glue. The all-volunteer Cedarburg Fire Department eventually became Cedarburg's "shadow" government since *all* of the alderman, commission members, and business leaders belonged to it. It was said that nothing got done in Cedarburg unless first gaining approval of the fire department leadership.

Central to that story stands Bill Ritter, who took over his family's soda factory from his father George. The elder Ritter had done the same from his father-in-law, who had started the business in 1886. Bill Ritter joined the fire department in 1933 and was made assistant chief in 1940 until Chief Schneider retired in 1963 at age 85 (having been de facto chief for the last few years because of Schneider failing health), and Ritter was finally promoted. He remained at his post until stepping down in 1978.

He guided many of CFD moves to make the city a safer and better place, beginning with the purchase of Fireman's Park. Ritter said in a 2002 interview:

Fireman's Park carried on the tradition of holding the County Fair on it grounds, as well as continuing the racing tradition. Proceeds from the Music Festival, County Fair, and the races paid for all the equipment the Fire Department needed, including a brand spanking new and very modern fire station, after 1928. (Photo by Harold Dobberpuhl.)

133

> We found out in 1939 that the county fairgrounds were going into foreclosure and being put up for sale at a sheriff's auction. There were $16,000 worth of bonds held on the property by local merchants, so we offered $12,000 to them for it to keep the fair here in Cedarburg and they accepted it. All this was done man to man, fireman to fireman, you might say. Anyways, we borrowed the $12,000 from the Cedarburg State Bank and then when it went up for bid in 1940 ours was the only one so we owned it from then on.
>
> To earn the money back we sold raffle tickets. That was illegal, see, the state had outlawed gambling years before, but no one minded or said anything. Heck, the bar owners said that the extra money they earned helped them get through the Depression and the war.

CFD resident historian Harry Wiegert said about the tickets in an interview in 2002, "Oh yeah, that was illegal as hell, but the bar owners got around it by not peddling the tickets—they just had the jars sitting on the bar."

Ritter delivered the "ticket jars" on his soda water route, visiting some taverns every day, "or they could come by the fire station to pick them up if they needed." The jars were full of 5¢ tickets, about $25 worth. The jars cost the barkeepers $7.50 and they kept the proceeds, out of which they paid the winnings. In further detail:

> If the ticket you drew out was red and had a zero on it, you won 25 cents. If it was blue and had a 11, a 22, a 33, or a 44 you won a dollar. White tickets with a 55 won 5 dollars. We made $25,000 in two years with that scheme. The state finally cracked down after someone snitched and we went to something else to raise money—we started with the stock cars and motorcycle races. Davidson of Harley-Davidson would show up [at] every race. The Milwaukee Motorcycle club ran the races, and we got a percentage of the take. The stock car races ran every week until Stan Roebken passed, and then they petered out because no one wanted to do all the work he did.

In the park these enterprising firemen saw that they had a cash cow they could milk for all it was worth, and milk they did. For 40 years, the city's Wednesday nights during summer would resonate with the roar and grumble of stock car engines; they could be heard all over town. Surprisingly, given that safety requirements for the cars didn't even exist, there was just one fatal accident. In 1959, Donny Klug rolled over after rear-ending another car and burst into flames. Over 70 percent of his body was burned and he died a few weeks later in the hospital. The only other fatality happened when a bystander was hit by a tire flying off of a car.

The proceeds from these races went to maintain and buy new equipment, as well as to build a new station house. The last time the city bought a piece of

Stock car races were loud, smelly, and dangerous. The crowd would see at least two or three collisions like this one on any given race night. The big surprise isn't that there were so many accidents, but that there were so few casualties. (Photo by Harold Dobberpuhl.)

equipment for the fire department or contributed to building maintenance was 1928. CFD also contributed vast amounts of time and effort collecting for the March of Dimes, going door-to-door every year and bringing in over half of all the money raised in Ozaukee County. The firemen regularly paid off mortgages on public use or non-governmental buildings; they made the last payment on the Girl's Club house, helped on occasion with the Peter Wollner Post mortgage, took care of the Boy Scout House's loan, burned the $5,000 note they held for the new city swimming pool, and generally extended their considerable wealth to any organization (and some individuals) that needed it. All the while they put out fires, even if it sometimes meant embarrassment for people. One day they responded to a call at a house of ill repute on the outskirts of Cedarburg (now the Farmstead restaurant). Upon arrival, the firemen were amused to see that they had not only got there in time to put out the flames, but also to catch a local farmer with his pants down. As Ritter recalled it, "There were plenty of laughs over that one."

The city slowly lurched into modernity. Autos had now virtually replaced all horse-drawn conveyances, while electricity extended its reach to more than half the homes in town and nearly one-third of the farms. Telephones sprang to life and the official services also improved their communications. While Police Chief August Frank served (1932–1944), calls for assistance came into the power plant. If they needed Frank, they would dim all street lights in the city to notify him to return. Later, when Police Chief Edmund Bienlein served (1944–1954) he would give driving tests, getting a quarter back from the state for each one. Keeping careful track of the amount, he finally bought the first radio for the police department, placing it in the jail, which still lacked a telephone. When a call came in, it went to the phone in the power plant next door and the person who received

World War II took many Cedarburgers overseas to fight for the freedom their ancestors sought. In this photo, navigator Bob Armbruster stands back and center with his crew in Iceland. This crew bombed several German cities in the conflict, returning safely from every air battle. (Courtesy of the Robert Armbruster Archive.)

it would then walk over to the unlocked jail and call the squad by radio.

None of the backlash against Germans that took place during World War I happened when the second war broke out in Europe in 1939. By this time, German-Americans had been fully assimilated into American life and, with the exception of a few farmers, spoke without even a German accent. The language was still spoken in homes and on farms, but not to the extent it had been 20 years earlier. Cedarburg residents also felt none of the ambivalence they felt two decades earlier. German-Americans in Cedarburg considered Hitler and his Nazi Party to be a militaristic and diabolical menace, a feeling enhanced when Germany invaded Poland in 1939. When Japan attacked Pearl Harbor a year later, a bombing that Cedarburg resident and navy bandsman Charlie Imbraglia witnessed, men and women from Cedarburg raced to enlist.

Sergeant Eilert Schuette, the city's first war casualty, died in 1943. Many from Cedarburg would perish and suffer wounds in the conflict's two theaters. Scores from Cedarburg served in the armed forces with distinction, including women like Lou Nichols, who served in the Women's Auxiliary Corps (WAC) in New York City. However, as far away and in danger's path as they might have been, Cedarburgers who went to war never left their lives far behind, as jeweler Bob Armbruster noted when writing home: "We visited a fishing village . . . went shopping . . . incidentally Dad, one of the stores had about 2 dozen alarm clocks made at LaSalle, Ill., probably by Big Ben. I would have bought one, but the price was too high, almost $7.50."

The war was a tremendous boost to the local economy. Factories made pants for servicemen, a dairy was converted to dried egg manufacturing, and Meta Mold Aluminum took over Hansen's Cannery site. Having gained many war contracts, Meta Mold operated three shifts per day behind a fence of steel mesh. Kiekhaefer also won many defense contracts, sealing its place as a major business force in town. In 1943, Kiekhaefer was awarded the Army-Navy "E" for excellence in performance of defense contract work.

Kiekhaefer faced down yet another threat to his business from his own board of directors that year. A group who held Kiekhaefer stock, the same "Takeover Five" from 1940 (Wiesler, Roth, Wirth, Becker, and the Cedarburg State Bank), opposed the proposed construction of an administration building in Cedarburg. They did it as a way to manipulate Kiekhaefer into buying back their stock in the company at inflated prices—and funding their scheme to build $100,000 worth of houses in Cedarburg.

The scandal played itself out publicly in the *Ozaukee Press* after a distorted and malicious article appeared slandering Kiekhaefer (a family member of the lawyers representing the Takeover Five published and edited the paper). Adlai Horn, the publisher of the *Cedarburg News*, joined with Willis Blank (who took over for his deceased father John) in publicly distancing themselves from the bank and the board members. Kiekhaefer replied with open letters and criticism of the bank and the community itself.

In retribution for what he saw as extortion, Kiekhaefer, who did $2.6 million in business that year, kept just $23 on deposit in the firm's Cedarburg State Bank

Carl Kiekhaefer is pictured here on the far right with officers of the Meta-Mold Corporation at a showing of new aluminum products. Kiekhaefer cut a wide swath through Cedarburg's business scene, but he hurt his family badly even while nurturing the community's economic growth. (Courtesy of the Robert Armbruster Archive.)

account. Additionally, when in 1946 he expanded operations, he built a new plant in Fond Du Lac instead of Cedarburg. The move to expand paid off handsomely, especially given the boost of post-war prosperity. In 1948, he introduced the Mercury Thunderbolt, a whopping 40 horsepower outboard. The Thunderbolt outsold every engine in the country and Kiekhaefer was selling $12 million worth of outboard motors a year.

His success in business, however, didn't translate to his personal relationships. He ignored his wife and children while carrying on an affair with his secretary. When his father died in 1948, he cheated his mother out of much of her inheritance by having her sign an agreement to sell him his father's shares for a fraction of their value within days of the death. The family protested and hired lawyers, but received only $210,000 instead of the millions to which they felt entitled.

Personal affairs aside, Kiekhaefer had again done for the burg what Hilgen had—put it on the map. Business was so good during and immediately after World War II that Kiekhaefer and others running factories complained of housing shortages. Hundreds of employees couldn't find a home in town and had to commute into Cedarburg to work. Stephan Fischer answered their concerns by putting a city-wide development plan in place.

Eugene Stephan Fischer's personal ambition all through life was to become an architect, but depression and his father's death, not to mention his large family of six younger siblings, forced him into commercial art. He was born in 1909, just months before his parents came to Cedarburg from what is now Croatia. His father was a cobbler, repairing shoes on the first floor of their home while the family lived above the shop. He took an early interest in community and preservation, attending many CAA meetings in the 1930s, and even convinced Dr. Wiesler to raise money to save the Gruntdke House from demolition. His preservationist instincts were sharpened by his experience in Europe and the Battle of the Bulge as a private first class in the 193rd Field Infantry. While there, he viewed with great interest the architecture and how the buildings hundreds of years old were preserved to be used in new ways. After the war, on a trip to New England, he became convinced that painting all Cedarburg's church steeples white like New England's would be an important first step in creating a preservationist attitude in town. He began with his own Catholic church, St. Francis Borgia. "I paid the priest of the church $50 to paint it white like the East Coast churches," he later told a reporter. He entered local politics at age 30, becoming an alderman and subsequently ran for, and won, the mayorship in 1946.

He lost the 1948 election, but had another run as mayor from 1952 to 1958 and a third from 1966 to 1982 for a grand total of 24 years. Fischer wanted to create a livable modern city in Cedarburg, and went a long way in accomplishing infrastructural improvements in his six years as mayor in the 1950s, including widening Washington Avenue; completing Evergreen Drive; extending and permanently blacktopping or resurfacing several streets; obtaining a full-time street-sweeper; completing and/or improving several parks; planting over 1,500 trees; building a new library as well as police station, utilities building, sewage plant, garbage dump; and requiring that all utility lines go underground. These are just few of his list of accomplishments.

Suffice it to say Fisher took the lead in overseeing tremendous growth that Cedarburg, like so many other communities, experienced after the GIs came home from war to raise families. By the end of the 1950s, all the streets in Cedarburg were graded and/or paved, the city's first subdivision, Westlawn, was developed and populated, new sewers laid, and electric cables put down. Cedarburg, which had 2,200 residents in 1940, boasted more than 5,200 residents in 1960—a 236 percent increase. America's building boom had hit full stride in Cedarburg, and it wasn't over yet. The 1960s would be the decade of white flight from Milwaukee into the suburbs, and Cedarburg would in the coming years become a farming, manufacturing, and bedroom community.

Forces of modernity would storm the town's stone bastions, threatening the structures painstakingly built brick-upon-brick and stone-by-stone. Yet, however hard Fischer worked to build a modern infrastructure to meet the growing needs of his beloved town, his greatest legacy would be his adherence to another idea, one with all the force and power needed to change the town yet again.

Stephan Fischer would move Cedarburg into its future by preserving its past.

Before the 1950s the streets in Cedarburg were all dirt and covered with a layer of tar to keep dust down, as this picture shows. With the advent of the automobile, however, new road surfaces were devised and Stephan Fischer saw to it that the roads in the city were black-topped or resurfaced with the latest technologies. (From the Rappold Collection.)

10. The "City With a Stone Face" Becomes an American Gemstone

Can an aging little city move forward by looking back? In most cases the answer is no. In a youth-oriented society such as ours, today and tomorrow seem to be more important than yesterday. But Cedarburg. . .Once a sleepy farm and trading center. . .is now building progress on its heritage.

–W.C. Nelson in a magazine article October 26, 1980

Everything changed when Turner Hall was demolished. Few residents saw the change for what it was, most believing instead that Cedarburg finally embraced modernity. After a decade of explosive growth that appeared would continue unabated, the city pulled up its Teutonic roots like a ship lifting anchor, steaming full speed ahead into the future. And the future was an expanse of shopping malls, service stations, and new streamlined buildings with large football field-size parking lots, not the blocky old stone things forward-looking residents of "the Burg" saw as cluttering downtown.

Turner Hall had been used less and less after the WPA financed gymnasium was built a few doors to the north. Complaints from students in physical education classes that floorboards on Monday mornings were slippery with and smelled of stale beer were memories, the balls of Victorian and Edwardian eras were but ghosts haunting its balconies. The Cedar Shoe Company actually manufactured shoes inside Turner Hall in the 1950s. Bob Armbruster recalls, "There were 200 women employed there at the shoe company across from our store. Business was humming then."

The shoe company left town for a modern plant built to draw them away from Cedarburg in 1956. Having possession of the deed, the Cedarburg State Bank saw the building as irredeemable and needing to be demolished, given the severe state of decay the former social center of town had fallen into. Besides, the bank wanted to construct itself a modern and streamlined building representative of its prosperity and leadership towards progress.

In this early spring scene, the unchanging aspect of Cedarburg is captured. The buildings in view had not been altered in almost 100 years. Some in the city felt that change might be a good thing, and they advocated tearing down and replacing many of these buildings. (Photo by Harold Dobberpuhl.)

Other stone structures or historical "relics" had outlived their seemingly useful purpose and owners wanted to tear them down and start over with bigger, brighter, and more modern structures. From one side of town to the other, a new age of growth and the American Dream threatened the architecture that the Teutons thought they had erected for the ages. The ensuing debate over the direction of the city split Cedarburg in twain. A newly-formed group, the Historic Restoration and Preservation Corporation of Ozaukee County, and later Stephan Fischer and the Preservationists, pitted itself against the Modernists, Cedarburg State Bank, and Merlin Rostad, the mayor at the time. Modernity would win the first battle but lose the war; and rather than become a clone of neighboring cities filled to the brim with large stores, huge parking lots, and businesses devoid of charm, Cedarburg instead would become world famous as the charming "City with a Stone Face."

Stephan Fischer had always played the political game from a disadvantage, due in part to his uncompromising approach. Those who knew him said he was one of the most stubborn men ever to hold city office. Fischer's retort? "Politics may be the art of compromise, but good government is not necessarily the result." But his own personality wasn't the only hurdle; he had to grapple with all the history of

Stephan Fischer is shown here in his prime, "Fischer's Folly" behind him and Cedarburg a thriving and vibrant preservationist reserve. His vision of a preserved and renovated Cedarburg stands on equal footing with Father Hilgen's dream of a Teutonic village on Cedar Creek. (Courtesy of the Tony Fischer Archive.)

Cedarburg. His brother Tony describes Stephan's first council meeting in which an alderman told Stephan, "I don't care what you want or what you say. We aren't going to do anything a foreigner and a Catholic wants." Fischer told a reporter in 1979, "I had three things against me—I was considered a foreigner, I was a Catholic in a Lutheran town where everybody was related, and I was a Democrat. Fortunately, it's not like that around here anymore."

Even so, while Fischer was mayor in the 1950s, he pushed through a series of civic improvements while critics scorned his repeated attempts to compel merchants to build new downtown buildings in brick or stone. Businessmen complained of the high cost involved and, seeing the dawn of a modernizing era, rebelled against "looking old" when they could present a fresh image. Some townsfolk dubbed these attempts at historic preservation as "Fischer's Folly" and painted him as anti-business.

Many opposed making the town a historic enclave by developing tourism, asserting logically that Cedarburg had no battlefields to draw people in, no famous personalities with which to capture imaginations, and no major industry to bring in onlookers. The only thing Cedarburg offered tourists were frumpy old stone and brick buildings.

Fischer, though, knew from his travels in Europe during World War II that the quaintness and architectural homogeneity of the town was unique in all of America, a fact evident to most who visited Cedarburg. One traveling University of Wisconsin professor wrote in the *News Graphic* much later, "You have in the six downtown blocks a most wonderfully preserved record of early Wisconsin architecture." Fischer was determined to nurture and develop that record and share it with the world.

Merlin Rostad granted an interview for this book in his contemporary lannon stone house. It sits atop a hill between Community United Methodist Church and Cedarburg High School on what is now called Evergreen Boulevard. Rostad is a sculptor and businessman, not necessarily in that order, with a forward-looking mindset in all that he does.

His contemporary sculptures, generally of heroic proportions and cast in aluminum at his plant in Grafton, are on display at institutions of learning and on corporate grounds across the nation. He came to Cedarburg to work at Meta-Mold in 1949, opening his own aluminum casting plant in Grafton in 1953, the same year he built his home on Evergreen Boulevard.

Rostad first ran for mayor in 1958 because he owned land that city hall had condemned along Evergreen Boulevard to create sidewalks leading to the new high school. He recalls two reasons for running: first the city attorney angered him with what he saw as a high-handed approach to the condemnation, and second many businessmen in town were unhappy with Fischer. He comments:

> Fischer was considered anti-business and I was considered a friend to
> business. I was strong for a change in downtown; I wanted to see a new
> street mall put in and other modernizing improvements. Even if you're
> on the right track, if you sit there you'll get run over. Cities must move
> forward to grow, they stagnate if they stand still.

Merlin Rostad, pictured here, ran for and won the mayorship in 1958 in a backlash against what many saw as Stephan Fischer's "anti-business" policies. Rostad would serve for eight years, all the while pushing for a "Modernistic" approach to handling growth issues. His efforts, unlike similar efforts in countless towns in America, would fail. (From the Rappold Collection.)

Adlai Horn, the grandson of Frederick Horn, ran the Cedarburg News *during the debate over Cedarburg's direction. Having a special responsibility as newspaper publisher and editor, Horn attempted to democratize the process of choosing between modernization and preservation. (From the Rappold Collection.)*

Rostad won the race overwhelmingly, despite Fischer's success in bringing infrastructural improvements to a town desperately trying to catch up during the baby boom years. "I did no campaigning, so the fire department [of which he was member] must have done it for me," he said. Early in his term, he employed Nelson-Ball & Associates, a city planning business, to float the idea of implementing a comprehensive development plan to revamp Cedarburg's downtown by making Washington Avenue a pedestrian shopping mall. In Nelson-Ball's report to the city council in late 1959:

> To strengthen the Central Business District so that it will continue to prosper . . . several improvements must be taken. The modern shopping center provides a physically attractive, convenient, and pleasant grouping of shops and services that can be easily reached by car . . . The district must be kept reasonably compact and oriented to the shopper on foot. Traffic through the middle of a shopping center is in conflict with the pedestrian shopper . . .

Despite cool initial reactions by many merchants along the downtown avenue, Rostad, factory owners, and the forces of modernity pushed forward for several more years, believing that this mall would act as a magnet to both home buyers and potential factory employees alike. On the other side of the debate stood a small group of people, mostly homeowners, shopkeepers and service providers, no captains of industry they, just people who saw the importance of preserving the historic structures with which Cedarburg was blessed in such abundance.

Adlai Horn, grandson of Frederick and publisher and editor of the about-to-be-renamed *Cedarburg News* (it would become the *News Graphic* in June), wrote an editorial in March of 1960 about Turner Hall, spelling out the dilemma:

> . . . a decision must be made to determine the fate of the old Turner Hall . . . Many are the memories it holds for Cedarburg folk—the minstrel shows, decorated in colorful streamers for proms and dances, sitting in the balcony, basketball games, the lone two shower stalls that home and visiting teams had to share, the crowded bar in the basement during public dances. To coin a familiar phrase—"those were the good old days."
>
> . . . The building is not feasible for use as a business or industry . . . For this use, architects suggested tearing down, with the lot as its principal value. Several groups are urging that the building be restored as a community project and used as a library and community center . . . Still another group believes that the city should be modernized; older buildings removed from the main street and replaced with modern structures and parking lots to attract outsiders into the shopping area . . . . What would you like to see?

Three months later, in June, a group of preservationists formed the Historic Restoration and Preservation Corporation of Ozaukee County by approving articles of incorporation and bylaws. Their aim was to "preserve, advance, and disseminate the knowledge of the history of Ozaukee County." Mrs. James McCray suggested that the newly formed group make saving Turner Hall its main priority.

Coincidentally, in September 1960, the Ozaukee County Park Commission voted to preserve the Covered Bridge, the last of its kind in Wisconsin, and still in use by automobile traffic. The *News Graphic* noted on September 21, 1960, that "The old bridge has been taking a pounding because of the heavy traffic, planks are loosening, and the only way to preserve it is to take the traffic burden off of it." The Park Commission decided to "move the bridge off its butments about 50 feet east where it will span the creek but will be used as a foot bridge."

Just weeks later, on November 27 of that year, the Historic Restoration and Preservation Corporation of Ozaukee County made its pitch to the Cedarburg City Council to save Turner Hall from the wrecking ball. A spokesperson for the group outlined a financial plan that included costs of $39,000 for the purchase and $142,000 for renovating the structure into a library, historical, and community center. Rostad recalled this from the meeting over 40 years later: "When the committee to prevent the Turner Hall from being torn down came around I said, 'OK, show me the money.' " But the fledgling group had not yet secured financing, and hoped the city would lend them official support and a promise of funding, thereby influencing people to contribute substantial sums to their effort to save the building. The council, with Rostad in attendance, lent unofficial support to the group, but voted unanimously not to undertake it in a civic sense and not to offer any financing received from an increase of tax levies. The council, in other words, said, "Good idea, if you pay for it."

A week later on December 7, the *News Graphic* published an article on a meeting of the Preservation Corporation where William Nelson, of Nelson-Ball & Associates, and Richard Perrin, a Milwaukee architect, both proclaimed the reasoning behind their efforts:

> Mr. Nelson spoke of the conformity of communities, that they look very much alike, and said he was enthusiastic about Cedarburg because of its individuality and character of the old buildings. He . . . told them not to lose heart if they do not succeed in all their endeavors, citing an infantryman's code of losing a skirmish but winning the battle.

In that same article, the *News Graphic* announced they were conducting a reader's poll to query the community's feelings about Turner Hall and the demolition. It asked readers to clip the poll from the paper and either send it in or drop it off at city hall. The ballot read:

> Turner Hall Restoration Ballot
> Are you in favor of restoring the Cedarburg Turner Hall as a county wide project, for a library, museum, and community center?
>
> Yes ☐   No ☐
>
> Name...
> Address...

> Please take in or mail ballot to City Hall, Cedarburg on or before Monday, Dec. 12th.

The following week, on December 14, the *News Graphic* published the following article:

> Drop Turner Hall Project
> Due to a lack of local support the Committee for the Restoration of Turner Hall have about decided to drop the campaign.
>   The ballot published in the News—Graphic last week brought in a large number of negative votes, and Mrs. James McCray, one of the leaders for the restoration said that because of the lack of local interest and support the project will undoubtedly be dropped.

In this scene we are reminded of the former prominent position that Turner Hall inhabited in the lives of Cedarburgers. Sitting next to it is the Cedarburg News *office; across the street and out of the scene stands Armbruster Jewelers. This site is exactly dead-center in downtown Cedarburg, a site which the bankers had determined would best suit their needs in a modern era. (Courtesy of the Robert Armbruster Archive.)*

> The committee also advised the Cedarburg Women's Club they not ask for a ballot of the membership, and that it would regretfully notify the foundations contacted stating, "That we have no local interest or support in completing our report to them."

On February 7, 1961, demolition of Turner Hall began. The building's walls were so thick and so sturdy that it took the demolition crew some weeks longer than the 30 days estimated to finish the job.

By the end of 1962, the Cedarburg State Bank was operating from its new modern/colonial building on the corner of Turner Street and Washington Avenue in the heart of Cedarburg. Rostad told me, "When [Turner Hall] was torn down I considered it to be progress. I've always felt that if you build a building you do it with all the tools and technologies and in the style of the day. Not retro—contemporary."

Stephen Fischer ran against Rostad in the 1962 election for mayor, but lost by a wide margin. He did not run in 1964, believing the city was dead set against his preservationist ideas. His attitude would soon change, though, on a day when his brother Tony came home from church with news that spurred Fischer to act again. Tony tells the following:

147

It was a beautiful summer morning, and I went to 7 o'clock mass early in the morning, the sun was streaming through the stained glass windows, Father Leo came up with a sermon and announced that they were going to build a new church in back of St. Francis facing South Washington Avenue and a year later they would tear St. Francis down for a parking lot. I proceeded to go home to tell my brother, you know, what I heard and what the plans were; of course, he almost, shall I say, had a fit? That's when he decided to run again, to do something about it. He could save the church.

Fischer ran for mayor in 1966 and won. His efforts as mayor were instrumental in saving the church, which still anchors Cedarburg's south end. He would be elected mayor seven more times, overseeing the transformation of Cedarburg from bedroom community to tourist destination before leaving office due to failing health in 1982.

What happened after Turner Hall's demolition to catalyze the community's embrace of preservation? An influx of former Milwaukee residents seeking asylum from the vagaries of life in that city's racially charged atmosphere, coined "White Flight."

The segregation of Milwaukee, perhaps as well defined as in any southern city, gave rise to racial tensions in the early 1960s that caused the pot to boil over into surrounding suburbs and brand new bedroom communities. People from all over the city, but mainly in the near-north side and northwest side, responded to the protests of Father Groppi and the riots that ensued by leaving Milwaukee for the "safety" of the suburbs.

The completion of I-43 north past Cedarburg from Milwaukee meant a drive into the city of less than 25 minutes. Contractors from 1960–1970 built subdivisions as fast as they could find materials; families occupied the houses before the final nails were hammered in.

Life in Cedarburg utterly charmed these new middle-class white residents. Seeing things through the prism of urban tumult gave them a better appreciation of the staid and stoic old buildings and the ever-so-German neatness they found in the town. A story, paraphrased here, describes how many came to view Cedarburg as the quintessential American small-town suburb:

The Lord God Almighty looked down upon the world and saw riots, war, hunger, and pestilence. He determined to locate and promote an earthly city as an example to all those world-weary men of how well life could be led on Earth, if only they would cooperate. He called on two of his angels most knowledgeable in Americana, Walt Disney and Norman Rockwell, and said to them, "I want a city that's solid, clean and neat, where everyone helps and pitches in, one that is pleasant, and one where they are as concerned about preserving their heritage as in building for the future, where . . ."

A bird's-eye view shows us what the downtown core of Cedarburg looked like in the late 1960s—and proves that the town had changed little in the 80 years since most of the buildings had been erected. Fischer's preservationist philosophy appealed to the newcomers fleeing the tumult of the big city, and these new residents led the charge to preserve Cedarburg's Teutonic heritage and building style.(Photo by Ed Rappold.)

> Disney butted in at that point, saying, "Say no more. Got the place already set up." Rockwell said, "Yeah, if it weren't there already we'd have to build it, but you're talking about Cedarburg."

Joan Wirth, who was actually a Horn and married a Wirth (one thing remained a constant into the 1960s, everyone seemed to be related to everyone else), in an interview for this book recalls, "In the 1960s we did become a bedroom community of Milwaukee's as the whites fled. The blacks looked like they were taking over down there."

Add the inherent safety of living in a small German burg, one in which everybody looks after their neighbor, and the place had special appeal to white, middle-class Milwaukeeans looking to raise families. Joan's brother-in-law, Gus "Sandy" Wirth who in 2002 and 2003 was chairman of the County Board of Supervisors, explains this story illustrating the safety of the town:

> Once, a lady in a council meeting, after hearing from the chief of police that we should be locking our doors when we go out, stood up and said,

"That's ridiculous. What if someone's car broke down and they needed to use my phone?" She had the total trust in her fellow neighbor that we all had in one another before the war and before cities got too big, he said.

By 1970, the desire to tear down and rebuild over the old foundations had lessened, in large part out of respect for the wishes of new residents, but some buildings were still endangered. The preservationist tide swept in, accompanied by a new tourism industry, only after a confluence of unlikely events in 1971.

The Wittenberg Woolen Mills had finally closed shop in 1968, leaving their huge mill empty and deteriorating. Now an empty shell with over 800 broken windows, the Wittenbergs wanted to get out from underneath by planning to demolish it and sell to a company that would build a filling station and convenience store. And so the forces of modernity reared their heads again without realizing they were about to be crushed; for Stephen Fischer and Jim Pape, a Grafton man, were about to deal modernity a fatal blow.

Fischer, having been made aware of plans for demolishing the mill, delayed signing the order authorizing it. He did so by telling then-city engineer Russell Dimick not to issue the razing permit, an action he later acknowledged was not exactly legal, or even within his official powers. It did, however, delay the property's sale until Fischer could find a tenant who would preserve it—that man would be Pape.

In this 1966 photo, Stephan Fischer shares a car with the other "mayor," CFD Chief Bill Ritter. The Fire Department played an important role in swinging public opinion behind Fischer's desire to create a preservationist attitude in Cedarburg. The CFD acted as virtually a "shadow government." (From the Rappold Collection.)

Jim Pape had married Sandra McCutcheon, another former Grafton resident, in 1966 while they both studied at the University of Wisconsin-Milwaukee (UWM). On their honeymoon to Europe, their eyes opened to the potential for preservation. Pape, while beginning his professional life as an accountant for Woolworth's, also bought old buildings on Milwaukee's east side near the UWM campus he converted to student housing.

Reading about the new interest Americans were taking in wine and winemaking, he founded Newberry Winery in 1969 with the first batch of Door County Cherry wine. He named the winery for the street on which his first home and renovation sat. He later expanded operations to a warehouse on Park Street and the Milwaukee River, making his own clay wine bottles styled after the old German bitters bottles with a handle on the small neck. "We made 500 gallons of wine a year, which we sold at $3 a fifth. We distributed it ourselves. The financing was so tight we'd spend a couple days considering a $50 expenditure," he said. The empty wine bottles today cost more in antique stores than the originals did full of vino.

Pape sought to expand again in 1971 and initially expressed interested in the woolen mill, but didn't want the entire complex because it was just too big for his small business. This is where the story becomes almost too coincidental for some people's comfort, suggesting something akin to divine intervention. An Arizona developer and preservationist named Bill Welty stopped by the Coffee Pot restaurant and asked about renovating old buildings within earshot of John Armbruster. Upon hearing that, Armbruster led Welty by the hand to the mayor's office and introduced Welty to Fischer within minutes of the initial remark.

Fischer saw the woolen mill's savior in Welty because he knew that Pape sought space to restore, but was near a deal at the more comfortably snug Cedarburg Nail Factory. Fischer went to the Nail Factory's owner, a Weber heir, and persuaded him not to rent to Pape. He then went to Pape and Welty with his plan. They would take over the woolen mill together and operate from it while preserving and renovating the compound. Together they negotiated a deal with the Wittenberg family that netted the family the same sum they would have seen from the demolition of the building and sale of the land: $55,000, or just over double the original cost of the mill in 1865.

Pape opened the winery in May 1971, selling home wine-making kits and a little wine as well. The shops on the first floor opened in 1973, with the second-floor shops opening a year later. Welty built a restaurant in the front (formerly the administration) section, selling out within a year. Pape recalled that the beginning for the complex looked bleak. "It was an unheated shell, the roof leaked, about 800 windows were broken. Part of it was boarded up. It was a very cold dank place." Although he did see rays of hope shining through the broken window panes:

> I thought that maybe the wine business would work commercially and give some functionality to the building and justify the cost of the renovation. Historic renovation starts with an idea of what the building

could be recycled for, and it goes from there. The wine business was perfect for this mill, bringing in people from around the area and tourists from even farther. When we opened the other shops, that only created more interest in tourists and day-trippers, and it snowballed from there.

The success of the winery complex was soon evident to other local businessmen. The respect he gained made Pape a dominant force in Cedarburg's business life akin to Father Hilgen in the town's beginnings. Pape bought the Washington House in 1983 and converted it into a bed and breakfast. His purchase and renovation of a stone house on Sheboygan Street set an example for other homeowners, one which only a few in the beginning followed, but most neighbors eventually embraced with great enthusiasm. Gloria Wetzel, a long time Cedarburg resident, said in a videotape interview:

> Cedarburg is more attractive today than it was when I was a child . . . the new people embrace the ideas as much if not more than the old timers. They looked at Cedarburg through new eyes and they saw possibilities for buildings, and they saw what could be.

Fischer and Pape became intimately involved in efforts by the newly-formed Landmarks Commission to gain Cedarburg entry into the State and National Historic Registers. In April 1985, the State Historical Preservation Review Board unanimously approved the city's motion to apply for National Historic District

This scene of Cedarburg's town square, with the Washington House in the upper left, could have been taken any time in the period after World War I. Jim Pape owns and operates the Washington House now; the Gerrit's Drug Store building in front of it is a Cedarburg Woolen Mills Shop, but the land in the background is now residential, not farmland. (From the Rappold Collection.)

As this aerial view of the north side of town shows, the Cedarburg Woolen Mill had been successfully renovated into the Cedar Creek Settlement, with two tourist buses parked in the drive. In 2003 buses must use the 40-acre Fireman's Park to find parking, and the scent of diesel fumes from the running buses permeates the weekend air to the north. Can a dowdy and aging city revitalize itself by playing on its elder status? Cedarburg has. (Photo by Ed Rappold.)

recognition. The Board granted the request later that year. It placed the entire downtown and most of Cedarburg's stone and brick commercial buildings (100-plus structures) on the National Register of Historic Places. This means that no exterior changes can be made that would alter the historic significance of the structures, although owners can do pretty much anything they like to the interiors. Additionally, the Wisconsin State Register of Historic Places lists over 250 homes and buildings scattered in the city.

Civic leaders saw potential in using the town's history as an agent for tourism and organized festivals, the Winter Festival and the Strawberry Festival to name just two, that would draw people in from across the country. These hugely successful events bring as many as 50,000 people to a town of 12,000 in a weekend. Tourism took off and remains strong. Buses from all over the country drop thousands of passengers every weekend, every season of the year. Docents walk the streets with crowds of tourists explaining the architecture and the culture of the Teutonic utopia by the creek, and historic events occur regularly at the Cedarburg Cultural Center. The Ozaukee County Historical Society raised money to renovate the old interurban depot as a tourist destination, museum, and historical learning center.

And so it was that the rescuing and preservation of the woolen mill once again changed Cedarburg, 107 years after its construction and 85 years after mill owner Diedrich Wittenberg brought the electric age to town. The woolen mill's successful makeover transformed attitudes in Cedarburg. Residents and businessmen alike could now see the value in restoring and renovating their predecessors' buildings. Artists and craftsmen flocked to the town to work and sell their products in such numbers that Cedarburg became an artist colony of sorts. Palmer Krueger, another long time Cedarburger, summed it up by saying, "People came here to produce and sell arts and craft—before you know it every building downtown had an artist or a craft person in it. We were different than other communities. We were on the go by preserving what we had."

Andrea Gyarmati, a youth whose mother works for the Cedarburg Cultural Center, collects and makes nineteenth-century women's clothing. She said, "It's just like walking through a history book, living here. Because I can visualize people wearing these clothes walking through this town. Some of the clothes I actually own were worn by people who once lived here."

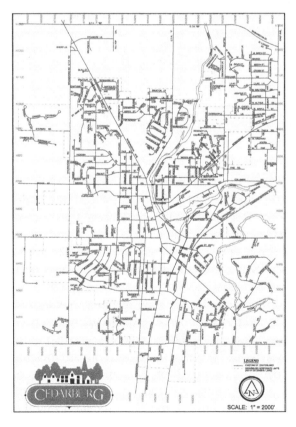

This street map shows that Cedarburg, while adding residential housing to the north, east, west, and south, has retained its quaintness with a downtown business district packed with old stone and brick structures through which one can walk leisurely on a morning. Growth advocates today cast an eye to the outlying districts to build business parks and residential housing, and no longer look with envy upon the downtown space—which anyway is off-limits by decree of the federal government. (Courtesy the City of Cedarburg.)

154

Walking through a history book carries with it certain responsibilities to future generations, as Jim Pape notes:

> You become caretaker when you are in a built environment and you have something like that to preserve, you really are caretaker for a period of time, because there aren't that many towns that are intact that have this much historic architecture remaining.

Gyarmati agreed, saying, "You really only get one chance at an environment like this—something maintained so well. And once it's gone, it's gone. Once you start tearing things down you don't get a second chance."

Today, even though there is vigorous debate over growth and taxes (some in Cedarburg would build industrial and business parks to broaden the tax base, with homeowners especially agitating for lower property taxes), not a single soul desires tearing down an old building to replace it with a modern one. The forces of modernity have succumbed to those of preservation, and the result is perhaps the most charming and livable small town in America.

Cedarburg in the twenty-first century exhibits all the same unshakable confidence in its path that their Teutonic forefathers displayed on their nineteenth-century route. The city knows it does the correct thing by treasuring their forbearers' traditions and buildings. Pat Rose, in her book *Small Towns of America*, wrote in 1994:

> There's an unmistakable energy in the Cedarburg air. It continues to be fueled by people who share a common goal: a commitment to the evolving and enduring image that is Main Street. Ten years ago, Cedarburg's downtown was fast becoming a memory. Now it carries the standard for what Main Street can again become.

Can a small town long in the tooth create itself anew through a focus on the past? It seems Cedarburg has. Cicero would say, if he were present today, that the town has avoided eternal childhood and come into full maturity by celebrating its past. In fact, Cedarburg wears its cultural experience as a badge of distinction. After all, the signs greeting travelers on their arrival into "The Burg" do read:

Cedarburg: Preserving Yesterday's Heritage Today.

BIBLIOGRAPHY

Apps, Jerry and Allen Strang. *Mills of Wisconsin and the Midwest*. Madison, WI: Tamarack Press, 1980.

Boerner, Richard A. *Art and Gladys: The History of Arthur Richard Boerner II and Gladys Adlyn Jordan*. Milwaukee, WI: A. Richard Boerner, 1978.

———— *C. Frederick Boerner and His Family, The First Hundred Years*. Cedarburg: A. Richard Boerner, 1989.

Boerner, Theodore. *C. Frederick Boerner*. Cedarburg: Theodore Boerner, 1937.

Cedarburg Cultural Center, *Cedarburg*. City of Cedarburg Landmarks Commission, videotape, 1998.

Corrigan, Walter D. Sr. *History of the town of Mequon, Ozaukee County, Wisconsin, Brought Down to About 1870*. Mequon, WI: Mequon Club, 1950.

Edquist, Nelson et al. *Cedarburg, Legend and Lore*. Cedarburg: Cedarburg Press, 1976.

Gedney, Sutherland and Katherine Pinkerton. *Bright with Silver*. New York: W. Sloane Associates, 1947.

Groth, Gustav. *In Commemoration of the One Hundredth Anniversary of the Immigration of the Groth Brothers*. Cedarburg: 1942.

Gruenwald, Myron E. *Baltic Teutons: Pioneers of America's Frontier*. Oshkosh, WI: Pommerschen Leute, 1988.

Gurda, John. *The Making of Milwaukee*. Milwaukee, WI: Milwaukee County Historical Society, 1999.

Haan, Beatrice Marie. "Settlement of Ozaukee County to 1860." Unpublished thesis for Bachelor's Degree at the University of Wisconsin, 1930.

Hawgood, John A. *The Tragedy of German-America*. New York: G.P. Putnam's, 1940.

Hess, Earl J. *A German in the Yankee fatherland: the Civil War letters of Henry A. Kircher*. Kent, OH: Kent State University Press, 1983.

History of Washington and Ozaukee Counties, Wisconsin: containing an account of its settlement, growth, development and resources. Chicago, IL: Western Historical Society, 1881.

Interviews with Bill Ritter, Harry Wiegert, Gus "Sandy" Wirth, Robert Armbruster, Ed Rappold, Robert Fuller, Jim Pape, and Tommi Faye Forbes. All conducted between winter 2001 and fall 2002.

League of Women Voters. *Cedarburg from 1841*. Cedarburg: League of Women Voters of Ozaukee County, 1966.

Kremers, Gerhard. *An Immigrant Letter: Manitowoc-Rapids in the State of Wisconsin, July 26, 1848*. Manitowoc, WI: Manitowoc County Historical Society, 1986.

Kuyper, Susan Jean. *The Americanization of German Immigrants: Language, Religion, and Schools in Nineteenth Century Wisconsin*. Thesis for Doctorate of Philosophy at the University of Wisconsin, 1980.

Levy, Lisa. "A Mayor Makes a City." Unpublished research paper in the Tony Fischer Archive, 1979.

Malone, John. *The Ginseng Growers' Guide*, Mequon, WI: 1930.

Magnussen, Richard. "World War Two Started All This." Los Angeles, CA: Unpublished thesis at the University of California Los Angeles, 1974.

McVeigh, Joseph and Frank Trommler, eds. *America and the Germans: An Assessment of a Three-hundred-year History*. Philadelphia, PA: University of Pennsylvania Press, 1985.

Pickle, Linda Schelbitzki. *Contented Among Strangers: Rural German-speaking Women and Their Families in the Nineteenth-century Midwest*. Urbana, IL: University of

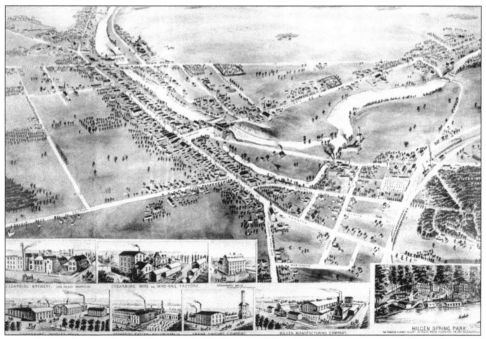

Much as the artist depicted here in the late 1870s, the Teutons who settled in and around Cedarburg had a very particular and neat approach to life. This impulse is called utopian when consciously attempted, but these German-speakers only knew subconsciously that they had an opportunity to create from the wilderness a place where they could live and work and worship freely. (From the Rappold Collection.)

Illinois Press, 1996.

Pixley, R.B. *Wisconsin in the World War*. Mequon, WI: Ozaukee County War History Committee, 1922.

Rauschelbach, Hugo. *First Immanuel, 1853–1953*. Cedarburg, WI: First Immanuel Lutheran Church, 1953.

Reichmann, et al. *Emigration and Settlement Patterns of German Communities in North America*. Nashville, IN: Max Kade German-American Center, Indiana University-Purdue University at Indianapolis, 1995.

Rempel, Gerhard. *Thirty Years War*. www.mars.acnet.wnec.edu/~grempel. 1999.

Rippley, La Verne J. *Of German Ways*. New York: Barnes & Noble Books, 1980.

———. *The Immigrant Experience in Wisconsin*. Boston, MA: Twayne, 1985.

Rodengen, Jeff. *Iron Fist: The Lives of Carl Kiekhaefer*. Fort Lauderdale, FL: Write Stuff Syndicate, 1991.

Rose, Pat. *Small Town America*. New York: Viking Studio Books, 1994.

Wells, Robert K. *Papa Floribunda: A Biography of Eugene S. Boerner*. Milwaukee, WI: BBG Publishing Co., 1989.

Wendt, Alice Schimmelpfennig. *Hilgen Heirs*. Mequon, WI: A.S. Wendt, 1988.

Zeitlin, Richard H. "Germans in Wisconsin." www.dwave.net/~dhuehner/germanwis.html. Madison, WI: The State Historical Society of Wisconsin, 1977.

Pioneer Village Review. The official newsletter of the Ozaukee Historical Society (obtained through the Wisconsin State Historical Society). Mequon, WI.

RECORDS, NEWSPAPERS, AND ARCHIVES

Public records, City of Cedarburg. 1885, 1959.

The Archives of Robert Armbruster. 1865–2003.

The *Cedarburg News/News Graphic*, Cedarburg, WI. 1883–2003

The *Milwaukee Sentinel*, Milwaukee, WI. August 19, 1843–2003

The *Milwaukee Journal*, Milwaukee, WI. May 27, 1918–2003

The Rita Edquist Archives. 1839–2003.

United States of America Census Records. 1850–2000.

Wisconsin Blue Book. 1952–1980.

Wisconsin State Historical Society's Digital Library and Archives. 1830–1930.

INDEX

Advent Church, 100, 111

Alt Lutheraners, 26, 30–33, 36, 42, 46, 48, 53, 104

Armbruster Family, 88, 98, 109, 110, 114, 117, 127, 129, 136, 140, 151

ausland, 75, 124

Belgium, 61, 77

Big Cedar Lake, 10

Boerner, Frederick, 39, 41, 42, 45–47, 50, 51, 58, 68, 69, 84, 102, 103, 106, 107, 109, 110, 119

Boerner, Arthur, 98, 106, 107, 109, 110, 111, 126

Bruss, John, 88, 103, 110

Calvinist, 27–30, 53

Catholic, 20, 24, 27–29, 58, 71, 73, 79, 94, 95, 96, 110, 138, 142

Cedarburg Advancement Association (CAA), 110, 121, 129, 138

Cedarburg News, 90, 97, 103, 137, 145

Cedarburg Volunteer Fire Department (CFD), 101, 115, 116, 133–135, 150

Cedar Creek, 9–11, 14, 20, 21, 36, 37, 73, 104, 110, 142, 153

Chicago, 17, 20, 21, 22, 35, 42, 66, 68, 89

Civil War, 25, 28, 41, 50, 58, 70, 75, 76, 79, 81, 82, 84, 114

Concordia Mill, 25, 26

Covered Bridge, 92, 93, 145

Cream City, 58, 81, 113

Democrat, 20, 55, 76, 77, 80, 104, 142

Deutsch, 26, 27, 65

Dewey Guards, 113, 114

Draft Riot, 78

Effigy Mound Culture, 10, 11

endogamy, 46, 93, 128

Fireman's Park, 101, 112, 133, 153

First Immanuel Church, 94–96

Fischer, Stephan, 122, 138, 139, 141–144, 147–152

fox, 12, 125, 126, 127, 130

Fredonia, 10, 77, 112

Free Thinkers, 57, 58, 63, 77, 84, 85, 96, 97, 99

Freistadt, 26, 31, 34, 49

Fromm Family, 125, 126, 130

ginseng, 124–127

Grabau, Johannes, 30, 31, 62

Grafton, 10, 12, 14, 22, 56, 61, 62, 65, 77, 80, 82, 86, 91, 112, 115, 143, 150, 151

Great Lakes, 12, 18

Greek Revival, 66, 67, 100

Green Bay, 12, 13, 16, 17, 20, 21, 24, 35

Green Bay Road, 21, 22, 31, 37, 43, 52, 83, 105

gristmill, 23, 25, 43, 52, 81, 85

Groth Family, 9, 36–38, 39, 50, 52, 56, 65, 69, 88, 94, 95, 115

Hamburg, 20, 22, 23, 30, 54, 56, 59–61

Hamilton, 23, 25, 26, 92, 96

Hartwig, Dr. Theodore E. F., 58, 59, 60, 65, 79

Hennipen, Father, 14

Hilgen, Frederick, 9, 38–47, 50, 52, 53, 54, 56, 57, 59, 62, 65, 66, 68, 69, 82, 83, 84, 89–91, 101, 104, 105, 122, 138, 142, 152

Ho-Chunk/Winnebago, 12, 13, 16

Horn, Adlai, 97, 103, 116, 118, 132, 137, 144, 145

Horn, Frederick, 54–56, 58, 65, 77, 83, 84, 86, 97, 62, 103, 144

Horneffer's Hotel, 58, 67

Immanuel Church, 94–96, 110, 111, 128

Indians, 10, 12–14, 16, 17, 35, 71–75

interurban, 38, 109, 110, 119, 154

Irish, 20, 23–25, 31, 54, 56, 62, 81, 95

Kiekhaefer, Elmer "Carl", 122, 131, 132, 136–138

King Frederick William III of Prussia, 27–30, 32

Kirchayn, 31, 49, 94, 96

Kirchhatten, 39, 40, 42

Lake Michigan, 10, 12, 14, 15

Lutheran, 26–33, 36, 37, 53, 62, 65, 68, 85, 93–96, 110–112, 119, 142

Madison, 16, 79

Masons, 78, 79

Mecklenburg, 26, 29, 31

Menominee, 13–16

Mequon, 10, 26, 31, 54, 59, 61, 65, 69, 71, 77, 88, 89, 95, 115, 125, 131

Milwaukee and Northern Railroad, 89, 103

Milwaukee River, 10, 12–16, 36, 37, 41, 52, 151

Milwaukee & Superior Railroad, 69–71

New Dublin, 19, 20, 23–25, 54

New Ulm, 70, 74, 85

Niagara limestone, 10, 81, 88, 100

Oldenburg, 39–41, 45, 50, 53

Ozaukee County, 10, 19, 21, 22, 26, 31, 57, 60, 62, 74–76, 78–80, 86, 88, 89, 91, 105, 120, 122, 135, 137, 141, 145, 154

Pape, Jim, 150–152, 155

Potawatomi, 13–17

preservation, 138, 141, 142, 144–148, 150–152, 154, 155

Protestant, 20, 27–29, 77, 96, 112

Republican, 55, 76, 77, 80, 104

Ritter, Bill, 133–135, 150

Rostad, Merlin, 141, 143–147

Roth, Edgar, 132, 137

sabbatarianism, 76, 104

Saukville, 10, 37, 77

Schroeder, William, 9, 38–46, 50, 52, 53, 56, 66–68, 69, 84, 90, 116

Spanish-American War, 110

St. Francis Borgia Church, 7, 29, 94, 95, 138

Trinity Lutheran Church, 31, 37, 65, 68, 72, 94, 95

Turners, 77, 85, 96–99, 101, 119, 133

Turner Hall, 83, 97, 98, 102, 115, 119, 120, 140, 145–148

Turn Verein, 85, 96, 97, 99

von Rohr, Captain Henry, 30, 31

Washington City/Port Washington, 19, 26, 37, 59–62, 72, 77, 79, 86, 106

Washington County, 10, 19, 33, 45, 54, 59–62

Watertown, 22, 65, 94, 116

Weber, John, 68, 87, 88, 91, 96

Welty, Bill, 151

West Bend, 19, 59, 61, 62, 106, 109

Wirth, J.P., 44, 95, 98

Wirth, Gus "Sandy", 130, 149

Wittenberg, Diedrich, 82, 90, 91, 110, 117, 150, 154

Woolen Mill, 82, 83, 85, 90, 91, 103, 110, 114, 121, 127, 130, 150–154

Wurttenburg, 32

Zastrow-Kussow, B.A., 56–58, 63

Zur Ruhe, 37, 94

CPSIA information can be obtained
at www.ICGtesting.com
Printed in the USA
BVHW010902070319
541922BV00028B/294/P